The Complete Web Assistant

Provide superior in-application help and training
using the SAP Enable Now EPSS

Dirk Manuel

The Complete Web Assistant

Copyright © 2020 by Dirk Manuel

First published: August 2020
Version 1, Print Run 1

Cover image © Gerry McGlamery 2020
`http://photography.mcglamery.com`

Print ISBN-13:   978-0-578-73861-1
Ebook ISBN-13: 978-0-578-73862-8

About the Author

Dirk Manuel is a Senior Consultant at Disys. He specializes in change management for large-scale ERP systems, in particular training development and delivery activities. His job titles have included Technical Writer, Training Developer, Training Team Lead, Knowledge Management Consultant, and 'the Enable Now guy'.

Dirk is the author of *SAP Enable Now Development* and several books on Oracle User Productivity Kit.

Dirk has a B.Sc. (Hons.) in Computer Science, and a City & Guilds in the Communication of Technical Information. He is a Fellow of the Institute of Scientific and Technical Communicators (ISTC). Dirk is a *SAP Certified Associate* for SAP Enable Now.

Dirk can be contacted by email at dirk@enablenowexpert.com. He can also be found on LinkedIn at http://www.linkedin.com/in/dirkmanuel.

About the Reviewer

Dr. Darwin Perkins has used SAP Enable Now since before it was purchased by SAP. Over the past 12 years, he has implemented Enable Now in more than 30 companies around the world. He worked directly with SAP Global Education to implement the concepts and training strategies for their Enable Now Partner program and still frequently talks with the Enable Now team. He has a B.S in Computer Science, an MBA in Entrepreneurial Business and a Doctorate in Business Administration specializing in Project Management and Leadership.

Darwin can be contacted by email at darwin@nextstopinc.com or by phone on +1.602.751.7401.

Acknowledgments

I would like to thank the great team at SAP for the help and support they have given me on my Enable Now journey. In particular I would like to thank **Anton Mavrin**, **Frank Störr**, **Michael Fritz**, and the true SAP Enable Now Expert **Jesse Bernal Jr.** for sharing their knowledge and expertise, and for their patience in answering my many questions.

Additional support

From the Author:

- Website: **EnableNowExpert.com**
- Wiki: **EnableNow.wiki**
- Twitter: **@EnableNowExpert**
- YouTube: **bit.ly/ENEtube** (case-sensitive)
- Book: *SAP Enable Now Development*

From SAP:

- User Community: **sapenablenow.com**
- Help Portal: **help.sap.com/viewer/product/SAP_ENABLE_NOW**
- Info Center: **enable-now.sap.com**
- SAP Learning Hub: **learninghub.sap.com**

Contents

WORKING IN MANAGER   125

WORKING IN PRODUCER   143

About This Book

SAP Enable Now is a software application that can be used to create and deliver courseware (including presentations and simulations) and in-application help. It consists of multiple components, one of which is Web Assistant. Web Assistant is an EPSS (Electronic Performance Support System) that primarily integrates with SAP's Fiori-based applications, including S/4HANA, SuccessFactors, and various SAP Cloud Systems.

This book primarily focuses on the Web Assistant component of SAP Enable Now. It covers everything from installation of Web Assistant and integrating it with other systems, through the creation and delivery of help content and the provision of access to learning content, to customization and ongoing maintenance. This book touches on other components of SAP Enable Now—specifically *Manager* and *Producer*—only to the extent necessary to support Web Assistant.

What this book covers

The individual chapters in this book together cover all aspects of developing and delivering in-application help using Web Assistant. Depending on your particular implementation requirements you may not need to refer to every chapter.

By chapter, this book contains the following information:

Chapter 1   *An Introduction to Web Assistant*
This chapter provides a high-level overview of what Web Assistant is, and what it can deliver for your users. You may want to read this chapter first if you are new to Web Assistant and want to learn about its capabilities before you start using it.

Chapter 2   *Enabling Web Assistant*

This chapter explains how to implement Web Assistant. Instructions are given for each of the major types of applications for which you can use Web Assistant. It also includes important guidelines on setting up your Workarea(s), which you should read regardless of the target application or your current system infrastructure.

Chapter 2   *Creating Help Content*

This chapter explains how to create help content for Web Assistant, using the *Carousel*'s Edit Mode. This includes the creation of Help Tiles, Link Tiles, and Guided Tours. It also explains how to provide What's New content. All Web Assistant Authors will find this chapter helpful.

Chapter 4   *Using the Web Editor*

The *Web Editor* is an on-line editor that can be used for editing help content and learning content. Typically, you will create and edit content via the *Carousel*'s Edit Mode, but some tasks—most notably embedding content objects such as video into Help Tiles—cannot be done via the *Carousel* and are most easily done via the *Web Editor*.

Chapter 5   *Working in Manager*

This chapter explains how to use the *Manager* component of SAP Enable Now to maintain content objects. As there are very few Web Assistant related things that you would need to do in *Manager*, you may not need to refer to this chapter very often.

Chapter 6   *Working in Producer*

This chapter explains how to use the *Producer* component of SAP Enable Now to maintain help content. It also explains how to 'extend' standard SAP-provided learning content into your own Workarea so you can customize it to meet your specific needs. This chapter does not cover how to create or change learning content (such as Books, Book Pages, and Simulations)—this is a much larger subject, covered separately in the companion book *SAP Enable Now Development*.

Chapter 7   *Localizing Your Content*

This chapter explains how to translate your help content into languages other than the original source language (which is typically English—the Web Assistant 'fallback' language). You will only need to refer to this chapter if you have a requirement to provide custom help content in a language other than the one in which it was originally developed.

Chapter 8	*Customizing Web Assistant*
	This chapter explains how to customize the appearance of the *Carousel* and the *Learning Center* to better meet your individual needs, or to match your own corporate color scheme or branding. It also covers some other things you can do to influence the appearance and content of the *Carousel*.

Chapter 9	*Integration with non-SAP Applications*
	This chapter explains how you can integrate Web Assistant into your own applications. This requires access to the source code of the application, and a working knowledge of HTML and JavaScript, so may not be for everyone. However, if you are interested in learning exactly how the Web Assistant Framework works, you will find this chapter informative.

Appendix A	*Web Assistant Parameters*
	This appendix provides a reference to all of the parameters that can be specified for Web Assistant, to influence its appearance or operation. Many of these parameters are used throughout this book, but this appendix provides a complete, easy-to-use list of them all.

Who this book is for

This book has been written with the following audiences in mind:

- Implementers, who want to get Web Assistant up and running for their company or client.

- Authors, who want to be able to create and maintain help content that appears in the Web Assistant *Carousel*.

This book has not been written for *learning content* Authors (who need to create Books, Book Pages, and Simulations). These Authors are respectfully referred to the book *SAP Enable Now Development*, which was specifically written to cover these things.

Conventions used in this book

This book uses a number of typographic conventions to differentiate between different types of information, and uses specific terms to mean certain things. These are described below.

Formatting conventions

Certain typographic conventions are used to identify specific types of information in this book. The table below outlines these and provides examples of each.

Convention	Example
Words that you see on the SAP Enable Now screens, in menus or dialog boxes for example, appear in bold navy. This includes all button names, field names, and menu options.	Click on the **Hotspot** button.
Screen names (including dialog boxes, panes, sections, and tabbed pages) are shown in navy italics.	The *Edit Tile* dialog box is displayed.
Web Assistant properties are shown in a non-proportional font (Consolas).	The `serviceLayerVersion` parameter is probably the most important parameter you will use.
Values you enter or options you choose are shown in bold.	Here, you can choose from **Always**, **Never**, and **Ask**.
System messages are shown in a non-proportional font (Consolas), in bold.	Wait until you see the message `Changes Saved` before continuing.
URLs are shown in Courier New.	Visit `support.sap.com` for details.

Additional information appears in the outer margins of the page. The following icons are used to differentiate between the various types of information provided:

● This is how a side-note appears.

● Additional information

■ Tips and Tricks

▲ Warnings

✚ Version difference

★ 'Advanced' knowledge or functionality for Administrators or Enable Now Power Users

Specific terminology

SAP Enable Now-specific entities are identified by initial caps, to differentiate them from more general nouns. Examples are Help Tile, Book Page, Hotspot, and Project.

The term "Author" refers to a content developer. The term "Master Author" refers to a lead content developer or SAP Enable Now administrator. The term "user" refers to the people who will use the help and training content that the author develops (sometimes referred to in SAP Enable Now as a Consumer).

Piracy

Please don't make illegal copies of this book. The author is an independent consultant, not a faceless corporation (not that *that* would make it any less wrong…). What little I make from this book (and I have endeavored to keep the price low) is unlikely to even cover the cost of the hardware and software I have had to buy just so that I could write this book. If you *have* obtained a pirated copy of this book, you can offset some of your guilt by making a PayPal donation to **dirk@enablenowexpert.com**, or Venmo me **@DirkManuel**. Random donations are also gratefully received!

1

An Introduction to Web Assistant

Web Assistant is the SAP Enable Now component that provides in-application help for web-based applications. Specifically, Web Assistant has been developed for use with SAP's systems running a Fiori interface, such as S/4HANA-based applications, which (most significantly) includes SuccessFactors.

Web Assistant is only one component of the SAP Enable Now suite, which also includes *Producer*, *Manager*, and *Desktop Assistant*. Compared to the other components of SAP Enable Now, Web Assistant looks and feels like an entirely separate application, and can be used more-or-less independently of (or without regard to) these other components, but you may find it more convenient to perform some activities in *Producer* or *Manager*. Separate chapters of this book how to use both *Producer* and *Manager* to perform specific Web Assistant.

In this chapter, you will learn about the types of help that can be provided by Web Assistant. Even if you are familiar with the Web Assistant basics it is worthwhile reading through this chapter, since it introduces the terminology used throughout the rest of the book.

● You can find a full list of the systems currently supported by SAP Enable Now in the *Product Availability Matrix*.

● In fact, Web Assistant effectively *is* a separate application, evolving out of an SAP-internal product called X-Ray, whereas the rest of Enable Now evolved out of an acquired product called Datango.

What does Web Assistant provide?

Web Assistant provides in-application help directly on top of the application screen. It does this primarily via the *Carousel*, which users can display by clicking on the **Help** button (the question mark) on the application screen. This button is present in SAP Fiori-based applications as soon as the application is connected to your SAP Enable Now system.

An example of a typical Fiori screen, showing the *Carousel*, is shown below. The *Carousel* is the dark blue panel along the rightmost side of the screen.

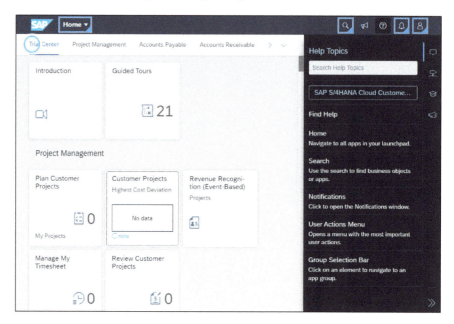

The *Carousel* contains up to four tabbed pages, depending on what has been enabled. These are selected using the icons on the far right of the *Carousel*, and are:

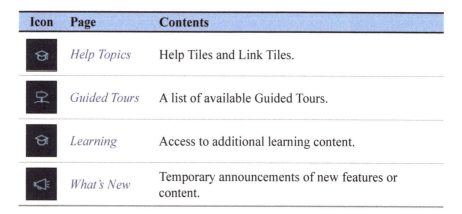

Icon	Page	Contents
	Help Topics	Help Tiles and Link Tiles.
	Guided Tours	A list of available Guided Tours.
	Learning	Access to additional learning content.
	What's New	Temporary announcements of new features or content.

We'll look at each of these in more detail below, so you know *what* you can do, and we'll then look at *how* to do this in subsequent chapters.

The Help Topics page

The Help Topics page is probably the most commonly-used page in the *Carousel*. It consists of a number of 'Tiles' (the vertical sections of the *Carousel*), each of which provides some form of help that is typically specific to the current application screen—although non-context-sensitive help can also be provided.

Help Topics button

There are two types of Tile that can appear on the Help Topics page: Help Tiles and Link Tiles. These serve different purposes, so we'll look at them separately in the sections below.

Help Tiles

A Help Tile is a Tile on the *Carousel* that provides short-format help, typically in relation to the current screen. A Help Tile typically contains a Title and a Summary Text, and if the user clicks on the Tile, a Help Bubble can also be displayed. This is shown in the example below:

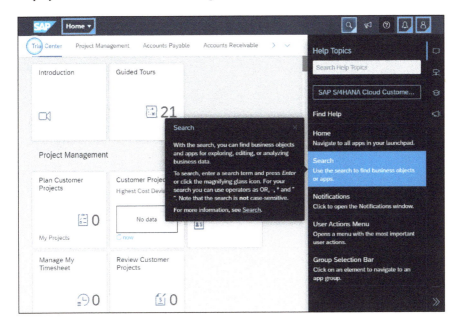

Here, the Tile Title is "Search", and appears in both the Tile and the Bubble. The Tile Text is "Use the search to find business objects or apps.", and the Bubble Text is "With the search, you can find...".

While we're looking at this example, note that the Bubble contains a couple of paragraphs, and a hyperlink. You can include an unlimited about of information in a bubble, but you should always be careful not to take up so much space that the user can't see the application screen any more.

One of the incredibly useful things about Help Tiles is that you can associate them with specific objects on the screen. Consider the following example, where a Help Tile is providing information about the Group Selection Bar in the application.

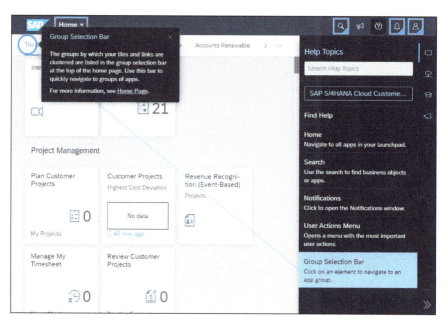

The SAP documentation sometimes refers to this line as a "laser" or "laser pointer", but "tether" seems more appropriate, as the tile is tethered to the *object*.

Here, the Bubble is *pointing to* the specific object to which it relates (actually, to a 'Hotspot' for this object—we'll look at this later), and a tether is drawn between the Help Tile itself and the object. The 'tether' line is displayed as soon as the user hovers the mouse pointer over either the Help Tile or the Hotspot. The Bubble is displayed when they click on the Help Tile or the Hotspot, and is hidden when the user clicks on either of these again. The user can also click on the **Close** button in the upper-right corner of the Bubble.

By default, a 'Hotspot' is identified by a circle (as is the case for the Group Selection Bar, in the example above). Alternatively, it can be identified by a rectangle, an underline, or even an icon.

Link Tiles

In earlier releases of SAP Enable Now. it was possible to assign a Hotspot to a Link Tile (and the linked content could be displayed in response to clicking on the Tile or the Hotspot) but this capability has apparently been discontinued.

A Link Tile is very similar to a Help Tile, but instead of the Tile providing a Bubble that contains (typically) text, clicking on the Tile displays a linked object. This object can be a Book or Book Page, a non-Enable Now file that you imported into your Workarea (such as a PDF or PowerPoint presentation), or even a website. This is a good way of providing additional—possibly external to Enable Now—information to your users. However, before providing a link to an external resource, you should be sure the link will be static for an extended period of time. End users can be very unforgiving when presented with broken links.

This linked object can be displayed within the current browser window (on top of the current application screen), or can be displayed in a separate browser tab. As you design these tiles, keep in mind how your end user works. Do they typically have dual monitors, or large ones that allow multiple windows to be opened? Does it make sense to open these links in a separate window that can be moved away from the application window, or would it be better to open the link within the same browser tab for compactness?

Below is an example of a Link Tile in action. In this example, the Link Tile links to a Book Page in our Workarea, and is being displayed in a 'lightbox' with sizing set to **Client** (don't worry if these terms mean nothing to you yet - they are covered in *Appendix 3, Creating Help Content*).

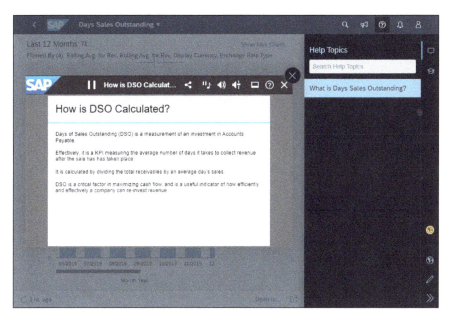

The Guided Tours page

The Guided Tours page provides a list of all Guided Tours that are relevant for the current application page. A Guided Tour provides the user with step-by-step instructions on how to complete a specific task in the application. It is possible to have multiple

Guided Tour button

Guided Tours for a single screen or function—for example, to cover multiple business scenarios. An example of the *Guided Tours* page is shown below:

A separate Tile is shown in the *Carousel* for each available Guided Tour (in the example above, there are two). Only the Tour Title is shown in the Tile (there is no Tile Text). Clicking on a Guided Tour Tile will launch the Tour, which will then guide the user through the task, one step at a time. An example of a typical Tour Step is shown below:

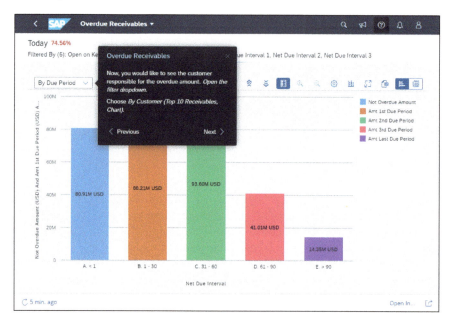

➕ In earlier releases of SAP Enable Now. the Step Bubble also included a Step Number and 'progress indicator' but these have been discontinued to avoid incorrect information being shown when optional steps are skipped.

Each Tour Step consists of a Bubble that contains the step instructions (Bubble Text). It can optionally also include the Step and/or an icon that indicates the *type* of information being presented. The Bubble may also contain **Previous** and **Next** buttons. A Step Bubble may be 'anchored' to a specific object on the screen via a Hotspot (just like the Bubble for a Help Tile), or can appear independently of a specific object.

Note that the *Carousel* is hidden when the Guided Tour is being displayed. It is re-displayed once the Guided Tour is completed or closed.

The Learning page

The *Learning* page provides the user with access to additional training material that is not strictly part of the 'application help'. Typically, this material will be Simulations or courseware (Books and Book Pages) which are provided through a connected SAP Enable Now Workarea (which may or may not be the same Workarea in which the help content is located). When initially displayed, the *Learning* page will display learning content that is applicable to the current context (the application page). An example of the *Learning* page is shown below.

Learning
button

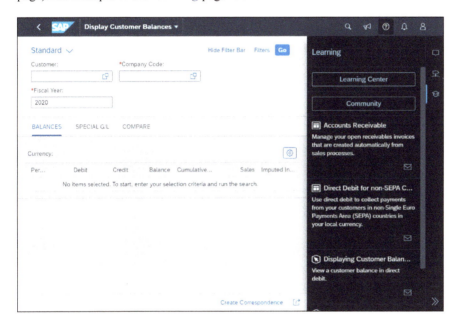

In the example above, there are three learning content objects available for the current application page: two Book Pages, and a Simulation. If the user clicks on a Tile on the *Learning* page, the object is opened in the appropriate application (the SAP Enable Now Book Reader, Adobe Acrobat, and so on) in a new browser tab.

There are two additional elements on the *Learning* page: the **Learning Center** button, and the **Community** button, both of which appear at the top of the *Carousel*. Let's take a quick look at each of these.

The Learning Center button

In the last section, we saw that the *Learning* page provides a context-sensitive list of applicable learning content, taken from the linked Workarea. If the user does not find what they are looking for in this list, they can click on the **Learning Center** button, and will see all learning content available in the Workarea—regardless of context—in a separate browser tab.

By default, this learning content is presented in the *Learning Center*, which is an easy-to-use interface to the Workarea. In the *Learning Center*, each learning object is represented by its own Tile. An example of the *Learning Center* is shown below:

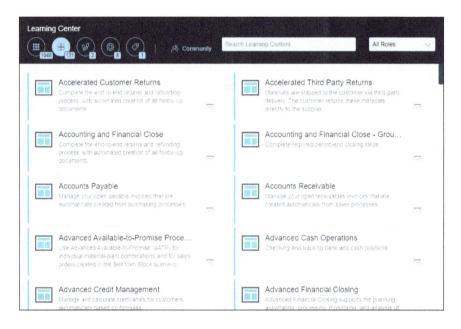

The *Learning Center* provides access to *all* additional learning content that is available in the Workarea, and not just the context-filtered content shown in the *Learning* page of the *Carousel*. If the content objects in the Workarea have been correctly categorized (see *Assigning Categories to your learning content* on page 161) then users can filter this content by category, via the **Show** option buttons on the leftmost side of the screen header bar. The number of content objects in each category is shown in the lower-right corner of the button.

Users can also use the **Roles** drop-down on the right of the header bar to filter the screen to show only content applicable to their role (assuming that content has been tagged for roles—see *Assigning roles to your learning content* on page 162).

Note that there is also a **Community** button in the *Learning Center* header bar. We'll look at this in the next section

As an alternative to having the learning content displayed in the *Learning Center*, the Web Assistant can be configured to display the standard SAP Enable Now *Trainer*, instead. An example of a typical *Trainer* screen is shown below.

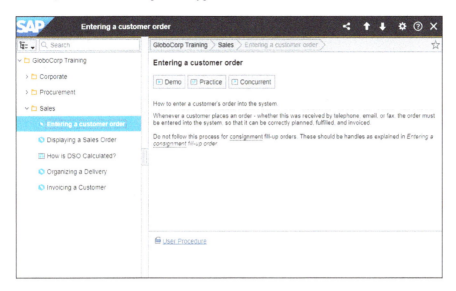

The Community button

The *Learning* page and the *Learning Center* screen may include the **Community** button (if this has been activated in the application's configuration). This can be configured to open a specific social/support community, such as a SAP JAM site, a Yammer group, or other shared resource (basically, anything with a URL). This is extremely useful if you have a culture of users helping each other out, or a strong Power User network.

User Feedback

There's another feature here that is worth taking a quick look at. This is the *feedback* feature. You may have noticed that there is a small 'envelope' icon in the lower-right corner of the learning object tiles—both on the *Learning* page and in the *Learning Center*. This is the **Send feedback to author** button. Users can click on this to provide feedback on the learning content object.

Send feedback to author

● In Edit Mode, the **Send feedback to author** button is replaced by the **Edit in Manager** button (which will pass you to the *Manager* component, and position you on the selected object).

When the user clicks on the **Send feedback to author** button, the following dialog box is displayed:

Here, the user can select a 'star' rating, and optionally enter any comments they have, before clicking the **Send** button to submit their feedback. Note that although the dialog box title implies the feedback will be sent to the Author, it will actually be sent to the email address specified in the **Email address for learner feedback** property for the Workarea in which the content object exists. This property is specified for the entire installation in the *Server Settings*, or can be specified at the Workarea level (which takes priority) via the *Workareas / Tags* administration screen. An entry is also created in the *Event Log* which is visible on the *Tasks* tab for the object in *Manager*, and will be included in the *All Learner Feedback Report* (also accessible in *Manager*—see *The All Learner Feedback Report* on page 138).

This feature can be disabled by specifying the parameter `LAFeedback=false` (see *Appendix A, Web Assistant Parameters* for details).

The What's New page

The *What's New* page on the *Carousel* provides a way to display content that has been created specifically to showcase new training, features, or functionality in the application. It works in a way similar to the *Help Topics* page, but has its own color scheme. An example of the *What's New* page is shown below.

What's New button

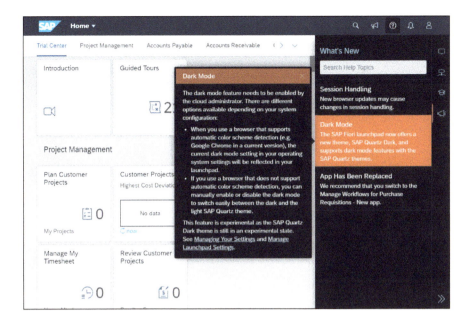

You can add Help Tiles (tethered or not) and Link Tiles to the *What's New* page, but this help content cannot easily be migrated from the *What's New* page to the standard *Help Topics* page. So this content should be considered 'temporary' content that will ultimately be deleted. This last point is important: you should plan on eventually deleting any content created under the What's New Tile (for example, when it is no longer considered 'new').

There are a number of additional features available for the *What's New* page, including forcing the *Carousel* to be opened on this page, or displaying a message informing users that What's New content is available. These are discussed in *Providing a What's New page* on page 92.

Where does Web Assistant get its content?

Now that you know what type of content can be displayed in the *Carousel*, it is worth taking a moment to consider where Web Assistant gets this content from.

There are two types of information that can be provided by SAP Enable Now on the *Carousel*. The first of these is what we'll refer to as **help content** and includes anything that appears in the *Help Topics*, *Guided Tours*, and *What's New* pages. The other is **learning content**, which includes anything that can appear on the *Learning* page and/or in the *Learning Center*, such as Simulations, Books, and Book Pages. These two types of information are both handled separately, so we'll need to look at them separately.

Help content

SAP Enable Now comes with a lot of pre-built help content and training material (for selected systems). This content is provided and maintained by SAP. This content is free, and can be displayed even without an SAP Enable Now license—all you need to do is activate SAP Enable Now in the application (as described in *Chapter 2, Enabling Web Assistant*).

● For a cloud implementation, all SAP Enable Now licenses are Producer licenses; for an on-premise implementation, Producer and Consumer licenses are separate.

Web Assistant can be configured to display [1] only the pre-built content from SAP, [2] only content that you have created, or [3] a mixture of both (with your custom content taking priority). Furthermore, assuming you have a valid Producer license for SAP Enable Now, you can modify the SAP-provided content so that it better meets your individual business needs. It is extremely important to understand these three scenarios and the differences between them before you implement Web Assistant. We'll take a closer look at each of them next.

The Extended Content Scenario

We'll start with the Extended Content Scenario. This is the most complex of the three, but once you understand what this scenario delivers, it is easier to understand the advantages and limitations of the other scenarios.

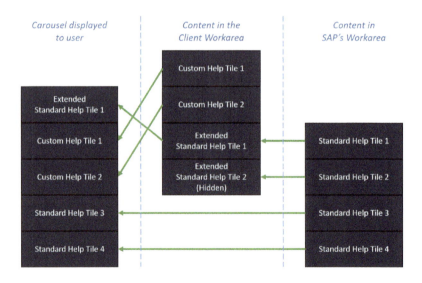

Using this scenario, the SAP-delivered standard content is available to you (as a content producer). You can choose to:

- Make the standard content visible to users (see Standard Help Tiles 3 and 4, in the example above)

- Hide standard content so that it is not visible to users (see Standard Help Tile 2)

- Modify ("extend") the standard content and then make the modified version visible to users, in place of the standard content (see Extended Standard Help Tile 1).

In addition, you can create your own content (see Custom Help Tiles 1 and 2) that is displayed to users, inter-mingled with the standard content (and extended standard content).

There are a couple of important things to note about this approach: Firstly, users do not necessarily know what is standard content and what is custom (or extended) content. This is generally a good thing, but you need to make sure that all displayed standard content is applicable to your client's system. Secondly, *all* standard content will be displayed to users unless you specifically hide it (or extend it to create a custom version). This sounds reasonable at first, but bear in mind that SAP may add new help content in a new release (and there may be no change log indicating that it has been added). This means that you need to be vigilant to check for new content after every release is implemented to determine if you need to hide it or allow it to be displayed.

The Standard Content Scenario

Next, let's look at the Standard Content Scenario. Using this scenario, all standard SAP-delivered content is displayed to users as-is.

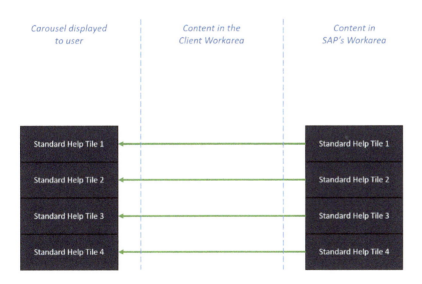

Here, there is no ability to change the standard content or to augment this with custom content. The advantage is that there is no development required (or even possible) on the part of the client. There is not even the need for a Client Workarea or any Producer licenses.

This is the default scenario, and is already implemented for several SAP applications, such as SuccessFactors—all you need to do is 'switch on' Web Assistant (we'll look at that switch in *Chapter 2, Enabling Web Assistant*) and you are ready to go.

The Custom Content Scenario

Finally, there's the Custom Content Scenario. Here, the SAP-provided standard content is still technically there, but it is not visible to you (as the content producer) or to the users.

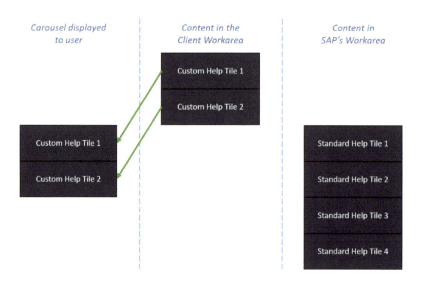

The advantage of this approach is that you know all content the users see will be applicable to them (because it has been specifically built for your client applications). The disadvantage is that you need to create *all* of this content; if you don't create custom content then users will simply not see anything.

Choosing a scenario

If you want to use the Extended Content Scenario, you should make this decision before you start creating any help content. For example, say you start using the Custom Content Scenario and create your own help content for an application page. If you then switch to the Extended Content Scenario, and 'standard' help content already exists for the application page, none of the content you previously developed for the page will be displayed . This is because when you edit the standard content (in an Extended Content Scenario), SAP Enable Now explicitly identifies the versions you create as 'extended' versions. When the help content is displayed, SAP Enable Now will look for an 'extended' version to display, or will display the standard version if an 'extended' version does not exist.

For reference, the three scenarios outlined above are often referred to by the following abbreviated terms:

- **UACP**: This refers to the Standard Content Scenario. (UACP stands for User Assistance Content Platform.)

- **WPB**: This refers to the Custom Content Scenario. WPB stands for Workforce Performance Builder, which is an old name for SAP Enable Now (it was renamed in January 2019).

- **EXT**: This refers to the Extended Content Scenario.

These three terms are actually values on the `serviceLayerVersion` parameter, but they are often used—both in this book and in the official SAP documentation—as shorthand for the three implementation scenarios, so you would be well-advised to commit them to memory, now.

Learning content

Where SAP Enable Now gets the learning content (that appears on the *Learning* tile and/or the *Learning Center*) is much simpler than where it gets the help content from. For learning content there is effectively only one model (not *really*, as we'll see, but it is best considered as *conceptually* only having one model).

For learning content, you specify a single Workarea, and which Workarea you specify determines the learning content delivery scenario (the equivalent of the Standard, Custom, or Extended Content Scenarios for the help content). Again, SAP provides pre-built standard content for some systems, and you can make this content available to your users. At the time of writing, SAP provides standard content for the following systems:

- SAP S/4HANA

- SAP SuccessFactors

- SAP Marketing Cloud

- SAP Integrated Business Planning (IBP)

Specifying a SAP standard Workarea as the source of your learning content is the equivalent of using the Standard Content Scenario for help content.

Specifying your own (client) Workarea as the source of your learning content. This is the equivalent of the Custom Content Scenario for help content.

Mimicking the Extended Content model is where it gets interesting. You cannot specify both a 'Standard' Workarea *and* a 'Custom' Workarea as *both* being the source of your learning content (again, you can only specify one source Workarea). However, what you *can* do is define your Custom Workarea as being *based on* (or 'extended from') a Standard Workarea. In this case, all of the SAP-provided standard content will be available within your Custom Workarea. This standard content will therefore be displayed to your users on the *Learning* page and in the *Learning Center*. And as with the Extended Content Scenario for help content, you can effectively edit the SAP-provided learning content to make it better meet your (client) requirements.

Although you can only specify a single Workarea as the source of learning content for Web Assistant, things are complicated slightly in that it is possible to specify a separate URL for the *Learning Center*. This is to allow you to have your help content displayed in the *Trainer* instead of in the *Learning Center*, in case you want to provide users with an interface they are likely already familiar with. However, it is just a URL, so you could technically specify any Website—for example, SuccessFactors Learning system, or even a SharePoint site or external knowledge base. Unfortunately, this URL only applies to what is displayed when the user clicks on the **Learning Center** button—it does not affect where the content that appears on the *Learning* page of the *Carousel* is taken from. This could be confusing if you specify a 'Learning Center URL' of anything other than the **Start** link of the same Workarea you specify as the source of learning content (as explained above).

Summary

The Web Assistant allows you to provide in-application help for browser-based applications. It natively supports SAP applications using the Fiori interface, but SAP are working to make it available for selected other web-based applications. The Web Assistant can provide Guided Tours, Help Tiles, and Link Tiles. You can also provide access to additional training material via the *Learning* page, and can also link to a 'community' website (such as SAP JAM or Yammer).

For some SAP products, such as SuccessFactors, SAP provides pre-built learning content that you can use and even edit.

2

Enabling Web Assistant

This chapter looks at how to get Web Assistant up and running in your environment. In some cases this may involve installing some system components; in others it may simply involve setting a couple of switches. The exact steps you need to follow will depend upon several things, including:

- The applications for which you want to use Web Assistant

- Whether these systems are 'in the cloud' or 'on premise'

- Your current system landscape

- How you authenticate

- Whether you want to use SAP's standard content as-is, or create your own

We will attempt to cover most of the standard scenarios, but you may need to perform additional steps or skip some of the documented steps, depending upon your specific requirements. We'll try to identify the points of divergence where applicable. There is also a list of additional resources you may want to refer to, at the end of this chapter.

Setting up Web Assistant is unlikely to be something you can do yourself, in isolation. You are likely to need help from your infrastructure people, the security and controls group, and in some cases, SAP as well. As an implementer, your role may be limited to coordinating the activities of other parties, but you should still read this chapter so you can communicate the requirements to these parties (who may have no experience of—or documentation about—SAP Enable Now), and ensure that all necessary steps are executed successfully.

As a final caveat for this chapter, the information provided here is correct at the time of writing (August 2020, and using the 2005 Edition of SAP Enable Now, and Web Assistant Version 2.4.10). However, SAP acknowledge that the process for installing Web Assistant is far from straightforward, and they are actively working to simplify it, so all of this could change. Always check the latest, official *Web Assistant Integration* document before starting.

Prerequisites

In order to extend and edit help content in Web Assistant, you must already have an SAP Enable Now implementation available to you. You can use the on-premise or cloud edition of SAP Enable Now, but it must be running on a HANA database (SQL is not supported). *Manager* must use HTTPS communication.

Single Sign-On (SSO) should be enabled in your system landscape. Several user-authentication platforms are supported, but SAP 'strongly recommends' its own SAP Cloud Platform Identity Authentication Manager.

Decide on your content delivery scenario

Probably the most significant decision you need to make before you enable Web Assistant is what help delivery scenario to use. This will drive many of the configuration choices you make. As noted in *Chapter 1, An Introduction to Web Assistant*, SAP Enable Now supports three different scenarios for delivering help content. These scenarios are:

● UACP: User Assistance Content Provider.

● WPB: Workforce Performance Builder, an earlier name for SAP Enable Now.

- Standard Content Scenario (**UACP**): Under this scenario, only the SAP-provided help content will be visible in the *Carousel*.

- Custom Content Scenario (**WPB**): Under this scenario, SAP-provided help is not available and you need to create all of the help content that will appear in the *Carousel* yourself.

- Extended Content Scenario (**EXT**): Under this scenario, the SAP-provided content will be visible in the *Carousel*, and you can both change this and add your own (customer-created) content to it.

The codes shown for each scenario (UACP, WPB, and EXT) are actually the values you specify for the `serviceLayerVersion` parameter in the Web Assistant configuration. These are a useful shorthand for the various scenarios, so it will be helpful if you remember the code for the scenario you choose to use.

It is important to understand that the choice of scenario above only applies to *help* content—that is, content that appears on the *Help Topics*, *Guided Tours*, and *What's New* pages of the *Carousel*. It has no bearing whatsoever on *learning* content—that is, content that appears on the *Learning* page, or in the *Learning Center*. You can choose to use the SAP-provided learning content, your own learning content, or a mixture of the two, regardless of the help content scenario you choose above.

While is possible to change your scenario after implementing Web Assistant, there are some additional considerations to think about. Although content is created and maintained in exactly the same way in all three scenarios, there are technical differences in how content created in a Custom Content Scenario is stored versus how content created in an Extended Content Scenario is stored. This makes switching between EXT and WPB (or vice versa) problematic— not impossible, but additional work will likely be necessary. Also, obviously, switching from EXT or WPB to UACP (the Standard Content Scenario) will result in you 'losing' any custom content (it will still exist in the Workarea, but users will no longer see it). You should therefore be as certain as you can be about what scenario you want to implement, before continuing.

Organizing your Workareas

When you first set up SAP Enable Now, you will typically have a single Workarea. This may be sufficient for you, or you may need to create additional Workareas—either for your help content or for your training content. If you do choose to use more than one Workarea, you should create the additional Workareas *before* you implement Web Assistant, as you will need to identify these Workareas during the implementation.

★ Technically, you will also have a **System** Workarea, which contains required configuration files for SAP Enable Now. This Workarea is (currently) not directly applicable to Web Assistant and so is not considered here.

Help content Workareas

If you will be implementing the Standard Content Scenario then you do not need to create any (additional) Workareas. The help content will be provided directly from SAP's Content Provider (CP) server, so you can skip this section and proceed immediately to *Implementation Summary* on page 33.

If you will be implementing the Custom Content Scenario or the Extended Content Scenario, then you need a Workarea in which to store your own help content. Here is where you have a further decision to make. If SAP Enable Now has already been implemented and you have an existing Workarea as part of this (typically, for learning content) then you could just use this same, single Workarea as your help content Workarea. However, because help content is (initially) created in the **Unsorted** group, it can quickly overwhelm other content in the Workarea. Furthermore, your learning content Workarea can grow quite large, and this could slow down Web Assistant response times as the Web Assistant Framework scans the Workarea for applicable content. It is therefore recommended that you maintain a separate Workarea specifically for your Web Assistant help content.

If you will be providing Web Assistant help in multiple applications (for example, you have an S/4HANA system and a SuccessFactors system), you may even want to have one Workarea per application. This will help you keep the content compartmentalized. There is no real *need* to do this from a user's perspective, because all help content is context-sensitive to the specific application so there is no chance of help content being displayed for the wrong application. However, if separate teams will be responsible for the help content of their respective systems, you may find that having one Workarea per application allows you to control who can change what (because Author access is controlled at the Workarea level).

Note, that you do not need to maintain a separate Workarea for different instances of the same application (for example, if you have separate Development and Production instances)—assuming the help content should be the same in both. In fact, because moving content objects from one Workarea to another can be time-consuming and cause its own issues, it is strongly recommended that you do not have separate Workareas for the Development and Production instances of your application. You can link the same Workarea to both your Development and Production systems—just bear in mind that help content created or edited in one environment will then be visible in all other linked environments—because it is the same, single set of content.

Following on from this, there is a scenario under which you might want to consider having multiple Workareas for a single application. In general, help content is tied to a specific page (screen) within the application, so users will only see the help content for a page if they have access to that page. However, there may be situations where you want different users to see different content for the same application page (for example, in HR applications where supervisors may need to see additional guidelines you want to hide from regular employees). In this case, you can create separate Workareas for the different user groups, and control access to them via separate application roles.

Creating a new Workarea

If you do need to create a new Workarea, you can do so by following the steps below:

1. In *Manager*, select menu option **Administration | Workareas / Tags**.

▲ You can change the **Name** later, if necessary, but you cannot change the **ID**, so choose carefully!

● The Workarea **ID** is sometimes referred to as the SID.

2. Under **Quick Add** at the top of the screen, enter a name for your new Workarea in the **Name** field. There are no limitations on the types of characters you can use in this name.

3. Enter a unique identifier for the Workarea in the **ID** field. This identifier is used as a folder name on the SAP Enable Now server, so you should

follow your server's file naming rules (if you are unsure, use a single word consisting only of lowercase letters and/or numbers).

4. Click **OK**. After a short while (during which necessary files are created), the new Workarea will be shown in the Workarea list.

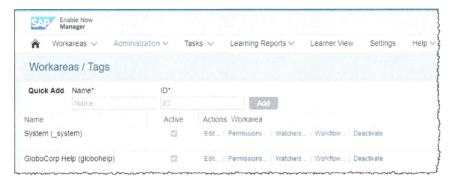

5. Click on the **Edit** link to the right of the Workarea name. The *Edit Workarea* dialog box is displayed.

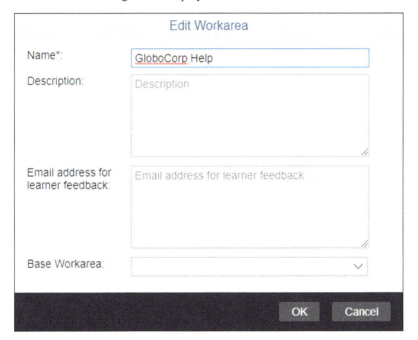

6. In the **Description** field, enter a short description of the purpose of this Workarea. This is for the benefit of Authors; users will not see this.

7. Enter the email address to which user feedback should be sent into the **Email address for learner feedback** field. If not specified here, the implementation default specified in the *Manager* **Server Settings | Email address for learner feedback** is used instead.

■ Strictly speaking, this is not required for help content Workareas as there is currently no mechanism for users to provide feedback on help content. However, that may change in the future, and as you should specify this for learning content Workareas, you may as well be consistent.

8. Leave the **Base Workarea** field blank (this is not relevant for help content).

9. Click **OK**.

The Workarea has now been created, and can be specified as the repository for custom (and extended) help or training content, later in this chapter.

Providing Author access to the Workarea

You need to make sure your Authors have permission to create content in your Workarea. To do this, carry out the following steps:

1. On the *Workareas / Tags* screen, click on the **Permissions** link for the Workarea. The *Permissions* dialog box is displayed.

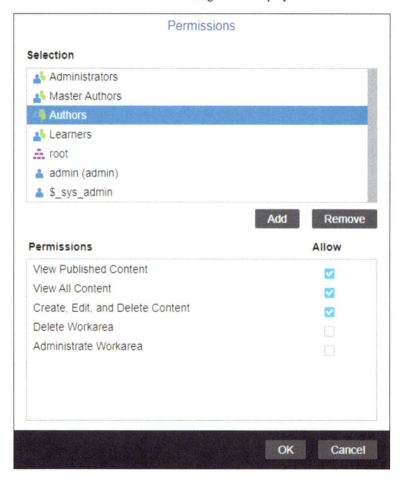

2. In the *Selection* section, click on the Role that you want to give write permission to the Workarea. Typically, this will be the **Authors** and **Master Authors** (or equivalent) roles.

3. In the *Permissions* section, select (at least) **Create, Edit, and Delete Content**.

4. Click **OK**.

Training content Workareas

If you've followed the recommendation of this book, you will have separate Workareas for your help content and your training content. You will typically only have a single Workarea for your training content, but you could choose to have more—for example, one per connected application, or one per project team, division, or organization.

The advantage of having a single training content Workarea is that it is easier to share and re-use content across organizations. It is also easier to maintain (and enforce) a single set of common styles, templates, and resources. The disadvantage is that there is no intra-Workarea access control in SAP Enable Now, which means that if you have a single Workarea containing content for multiple organizations, any Author in any organization can change the content for any other organization.

One final consideration when deciding whether to have one or multiple Workareas, and this is specific to Web Assistant: you can only link a single learning content Workarea to the *Learning* page and *Learning Center*. This means that all of the learning content you want to be accessible within a given application must be contained in a single Workarea (although you can always create a Link Tile or text link to provide access to content in another Workarea).

You can create additional Workareas for your training content as explained in *Creating a new Workarea* on page 26.

Connecting a standard Workarea

As we saw in *Chapter 1, An Introduction to Web Assistant*, SAP provides pre-built content for an ever-increasing number of its applications, including S/4HANA and SuccessFactors. You have full access to this content, and can link it into your own *Manager* implementation. Linked Workareas are read-only, but as we shall see later, it is possible to take copies of this content and then change the copy.

★ A Connected Workarea is effectively a mirror of the official SAP-maintained Workarea. How often this is refreshed with any new or updated content is defined via the Server Administration **Connected workarea | Connected Workarea Synchronize Time** setting.

To connect one of the SAP-provided standard Workareas to your *Manager*, carry out the following steps.

1. Log on to *Manager*.

2. Select menu option **Administration | Workareas / Tags**.

3. Click the **Connect** button on the upper-right of the *Workareas / Tags* screen, just under the text **Connected workarea from Manager**. The *Connect to Workarea on Manager* dialog box is displayed.

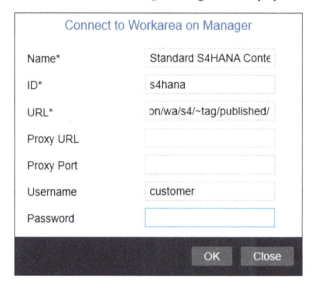

★ If you do not see the **Connect** button, ask your Administrator to select the **Enable Connected Workarea Feature** option in **Server Settings**.

4. In the **Name** field, enter a suitable name for the Workarea you want to connect. This can be anything, and is solely for your own reference; it will not be seen by users, but you may want to include the text "Connected" as a reminder for your Authors.

5. In the **ID** field, enter a technical identifier for the Workarea. Again, you can choose any value here, but it should be a short single-word text string with no special characters in it. You may choose to use the same ID as SAP uses (see the table in Step 6) to keep things clear, possibly appending "_Connected" to it.

6. In the **URL** field, enter the full URL of the standard Workarea that you are connecting. This will depend on the application to which the Workarea relates, but will be in the format:

```
https://education.hana.ondemand.com/education/wa/
{system}/~tag/published/
```

where *{system}* is as follows:

Application	*{system}*
S/4HANA	s4
SAP CRM	c4
SAP IBP	Digi_Manf_Cld (case sensitive!)
SAP SuccessFactors	sfsf

7. If you use an internal proxy server, specify the URL of this in the **Proxy URL** field, and the port number in the **Proxy Port** field.

8. Enter a **Username** of **customer** (always, in all cases).

9. Leave the **Password** field blank.

10. Click **OK**.

It may take 20-30 minutes for the Workarea to be connected. Occasionally this will fail with an error message; just refresh the browser window and try again. Once the connection has been successfully established, the connected Workarea will be listed on the *Workareas / Tags* screen, with a purple "**Connected**" indicator after the Workarea name, as shown below.

You can now access this Workarea just like you would any of your own Workareas, in *Manager* or *Producer*—bearing in mind that it is read-only. You can even make the content in this Workarea available to your users via Web Assistant. If you are using an Extended Content Scenario, you can change the content in the **Connected** Workarea, but to do this, you need to 'extend' it to a Workarea of your own, so you can pull content from the **Connected** Workarea into your own Workarea, and change it there. How to set this up is covered in the next section.

Extending a standard Workarea

Once you have one of the SAP-provided standard Workareas connected to your *Manager*, you can extend it to a Workarea of your own. You do this by specifying your own Workarea as being 'based on' the standard Workarea. To do this, carry out the steps shown below.

● This is sometimes referred to as a 'Workarea overlay'.

1. On the *Tags / Workareas* screen, locate an existing Workarea of your own (or create a new one) that you want to have access to a **Connected** Workarea.

GlóboCorp (globocorp)   Edit... | Permissions...

2. Click on the **Edit** link. The *Edit Workarea* dialog box is displayed.

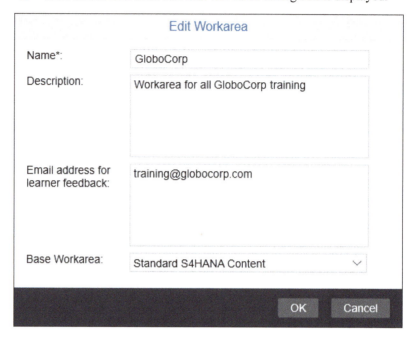

Edit Workarea

Name*: GloboCorp

Description: Workarea for all GloboCorp training

Email address for learner feedback: training@globocorp.com

Base Workarea: Standard S4HANA Content

OK   Cancel

★ If you do not see the **Base Workarea** field, ask your Administrator to select the **Enable Workarea Extensibility Feature** option in **Server Settings**.

3. In the **Base Workarea** field, select the standard Workarea (that you have already connected) that you want your own Workarea to be based on, from the drop-down list.

4. Click **OK**.

Your Workarea will now be listed as being 'extended' from another Workarea, as shown in the example below.

GloboCorp (globocorp) **EXTENDED**   Edit... | Permissions...

All of the content in the **Connected** Workarea is now accessible from your own **Extended** Workarea. It will be visible in both *Manager* and *Producer*, where it will be flagged with an orange dot (although a purple dot would be more logical). Most significantly, if you set your Workarea as being the source for learning content in Web Assistant, your users will see the standard content as well as your custom content, both on the *Learning* page and in the *Learning Center*.

This content will initially appear under **Unsorted**, but you can move it to any other location within your Workarea, as necessary. In fact, it is advisable to move (only) the content applicable to your specific application and version to somewhere in your **Root**—especially if you will use the *Trainer* as your *Learning Center* (see *Including standard content in the Trainer* on page 163).

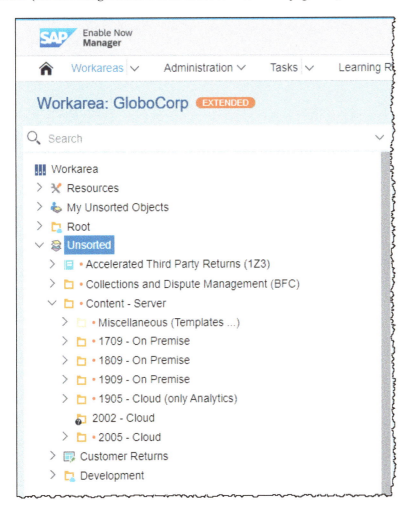

Content in the Connected (SAP-provided) Workarea is read-only and cannot be edited. However, you can 'extend' it into your own Workarea, and then change it there. How to do this in *Manager* is explained in *Changing standard learning content in Manager* on page 130, and how to do so in *Producer* is explained in *Changing standard training content in Producer* on page 150.

Implementation Summary

There are several steps that must be carried out to set up Web Assistant. Some of these are common to each scenario, and some are unique. The table below summarizes these steps and provides the page number of each applicable section. You should refer only to those sections that apply to your specific scenario.

Action	S/4HANA On Premise	S/4HANA Cloud	SAP Cloud Platform	SuccessFactors	See Page
Set up your Workarea	●	●	●	●	25
Enable SSO authorization	●	●	●	●	34
Set up Web Dispatcher	●				36
Add a Fiori Catalog and define the Web Assistant plugin	●				41
Define Communications for S/4HANA Cloud		●			47
Create a Cloud plugin			●		50
Set up Web Assistant in SuccessFactors				●	52
Define Trusted Sites in the Browser	●	●	●	●	54
Activate CORS	●	●	●	●	54

Enabling SSO Authentication

You should enable Single Sign-On for your SAP Enable Now implementation. Otherwise, users will be prompted to log onto Web Assistant every time they access the target application—even after they have already logged on to the application (because SAP Enable Now is a separate application with its own user access control). You should also make sure that authorization for the target application (for which you are providing help) and your SAP Enable Now application both use the same IAS tenant. This is necessary so that once the user is authenticated against the application, the SAML token issued by the IAS tenant will also be valid for SAP Enable Now.

● IAS: Identity Authorization Service. SAML: Security Assertion Markup Language.

This is one of the areas where you will certainly need help. Contact the person or group responsible for system security, and make sure they are part of this process—they may want to perform these steps for you. Ask them what Identity Provider is being used—SAP will want to know this information. Your Identity Provider is likely to be one of Microsoft ADFS (Active Directory Federation Services), Microsoft Azure, Okta, or Ping Federation. Which flavor of Identity Provider is used does not really matter (but see below), as long as it is SAML-compliant. You will then need to open an Incident with SAP, requesting a meeting to enable SSO. Specify component **KM_WPB-MGR** in the Incident. You should make sure the following people from, within your organization attend the meeting:

● You can open an incident from `support.sap.com`. You will need an S* ID to do this.

- SAP Enable Now Administrator (this may be you)

- IAS Administrator
- SAML Identity Provider Administrator
- A non-Admin user who can test the set-up

If all of these people attend the meeting—and they have the access they need to configure their various components (this is critical!)—SAP will be able to guide you through the steps necessary to set up SSO access for Web Assistant. If everything goes well, you should have SSO set up by the end of the meeting.

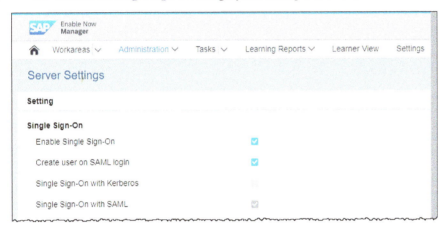

Bear in mind that the SAP resources who will attend are typically located in Europe, so you should schedule the (1-hour) meeting to take place during European work hours.

Before this meeting, you should set up your SAP Enable Now system so it is ready to support SSO. Do this as follows:

1. Log on to *Manager*.

2. Select menu option **Administration | Server Settings**.

3. Locate the *Single Sign-On* category. An example of this is shown below:

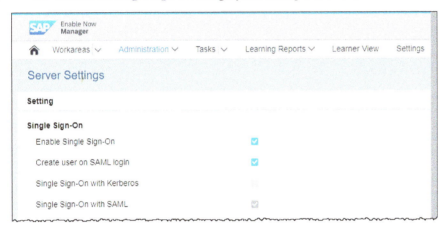

4. Make the following changes:

    ♦ Select the **Enable Single Sign-On** checkbox.

    ♦ Select the **Create user on SAML login** checkbox. This will create a Userid for the user in SAP Enable Now when they first attempt to access your help or training content. This is automatic and transparent to the user.

5. Click **Save** to save your changes.

Additional help on setting up SSO can be found in the SAP Knowledge Base, articles **2823440** and **2715476**.

Additional parameters for SSO

Some Identity Providers, including Microsoft Azure and Okta do not allow SAML authorization in iFrames, which is the default run state for SAP Enable

Now. To work around this, Web Assistant can be configured to open a new browser window in which to perform the authentication (this window is then closed as soon as authentication is complete). To enable this configuration, enter the following parameter in the Web Assistant settings:

```
newWindowSAML=true
```

You will also need to disable any browser pop-up blocker (at least for the target application) so this additional window can be opened.

Setting up Web Dispatcher

Web Dispatcher only needs to be set up for On-Premise S/4HANA systems, but is required for all content delivery scenarios.

★ It is possible to use a customer proxy server instead of Web Dispatcher, as long as this is configured to meet the requirements of Web Assistant as explained in this section.

SAP Web Dispatcher is a reverse-proxy server that sits between the Internet and the on=premise S/4HANA system, in the DMZ (the 'De-Militarized Zone' - effectively on the outside of a company's firewall). It is the entry point for HTTP(s) requests into your system, and can accept or reject connections, routing requests between the S/4HANA application and (for our purposes) the Web Assistant servers.

You only need one Web Dispatcher in your system landscape; it can perform its duties for multiple S/4HANA or NetWeaver systems. You should therefore check if it has already been installed in your system landscape. If Web Dispatcher is already installed and available you can skip Step 1 below, but you will still need to perform Step 2 onward as those steps are specific to SAP Enable Now.

If you *are* using an existing Web Assistant, you should confirm that it can access the following URLs:

```
https://cp.hana.ondemand.com
https://xray.hana.ondemand.com
```

The Future of Web Dispatcher

It is widely expected that the requirement to use Web Dispatcher will be removed in a future release of SAP Enable Now—most likely in the 20.11 release (November 2020). It is largely needed to allow the Web Assistant Framework—which exists on SAP's own servers—to be accessed. The plan is for this Framework to be provided within SAP Enable Now itself, as a Resource in the System Workarea. Once this happens, it will only be necessary to specify the URL of this resource in the **resourceUrl** parameter, and Web Dispatcher will no longer be required. Before setting up Web Dispatcher, please check the *Web Assistant Integration Guide* for your SAP Enable Now version to see if this change has been implemented.

Step 1: Install Web Dispatcher

Installing Web Dispatcher is not normally something that is done by the SAP Enable Now consultant or Administrator. It is usually done by the system support team. Therefore, it is not covered in detail here. However, if you do need to install Web Assistant yourself, you can locate detailed instructions as follows:

1. Navigate to the *SAP Help Portal* at `http://help.sap.com/viewer/p/SAP_NETWEAVER_AS_ABAP_752` (substitute "752" for the appropriate version as necessary).

2. In the *Application Help* section, select **SAP NetWeaver Library: Function-Oriented View**.

3. In the *Table of Contents* on the left, navigate to and select:
    > SAP NetWeaver Application Server for ABAP Infrastructure
    > Components of SAP NetWeaver Application Server for ABAP
    > SAP Web Dispatcher.

4. Under *Related Information* select **Administration of the SAP Web Dispatcher**.

5. Under *Related Information* select **Operating SAP Web Dispatcher**.

6. Under *Related Information* select **Installing SAP Web Dispatcher**.

Follow the instructions on the *Installing SAP Web Dispatcher* page.

● This path is correct as of the time of writing, but could change if SAP reorganizes the content again. If you can't find the instructions here, start from the *SAP Fiori: Setup and Configuration Guide* and look for the section on installing Web Dispatcher.

Step 2: Create a redirect page

You need to create a 'redirect page' which will redirect requests from the S/4HANA system to the Web Assistant servers.

To do this, create a simple text file called `redirect.txt`, with the following contents:

```
# User Assistance Content Platform - rewrite rule
if %{SID} = WA1
begin
SetHeader HOST cp.hana.ondemand.com
RegRewriteRawUrl ^/sap/dfa/help/(.*) /dps/$1
end
# Script Server - rewrite rule
if %{SID} = WA2
begin
SetHeader HOST xray.hana.ondemand.com
RegRewriteRawUrl ^/resources/sap/dfa/help/(.*) /
xRayControls/resources/sap/dfa/help/$1
end
```

▲ Make sure you enter this text exactly shown here, and that there is no blank line at the end of the file.

The only thing you can change here is the text in red (WA1 and WA2), but if you change them here, you also need to change them in additional places below, so for simplicity it may be better to just leave them as specified above. For reference, WA1 points to the Content Provider (CP) Server, which contains all of the standard SAP-provided help content, and WA2 points to the Web Assistant Server, which provides the Web Assistant Framework.

Once you have created this file, load it into the following directory on your Web Dispatcher:

```
sapmnt/ssl/profile
```

Next, open the Web Dispatcher instance profile (`sapwebdisp.pf`), and **add** the following entries to it:

```
# Web Assistant Setings----------------------------------
wdisp/system_conflict_resolution=FIRST_MATCH icm/HTTP/
mod_0=PREFIX=/, FILE=$(DIR_PROFILE)/redirect.txt

# Web Assistant Back-end system configuration ------------
# Added for Web Assistant SID= WA1/WA2 dummy sids
wdisp/system_0 = SID=WA1, EXTSRV=https://cp.hana.
ondemand.com,PROXY=proxy.globocorp.com:8080, SRCURL=/sap/
dfa/help/, SRCSRV=*:*, STANDARD_COOKIE_FILTER=OFF

wdisp/system_1 = SID=WA2, EXTSRV=https://xray.hana.
ondemand.com,PROXY=proxy.globocorp.com:8080, SRCURL=/
resources/sap/dfa/help/, SRCSRV=*:*, STANDARD_COOKIE_
FILTER=OFF
```

Here, you should specify your own proxy server on the PROXY parameter (or delete this parameter if you do not have your own proxy server). You should also make sure that the SIDs specified here match those specified in the redirect page.

Do not log off from Web Dispatcher, yet—you need to be logged on for the next step.

You can test that the SAP content server redirect is working correctly by connecting to:

```
https://webdispatcher:port/sap/dfa/help/odata.
svc/?$format=json
```

where *webdispatcher:port* is the URL and port of your Web Dispatcher.

If everything is OK, you will see a response of:

```
{"d":{"EntitySets":["Transport","DeliverableForRep
lication","Tile","Project","Deliverable","Transpor
tHistory","TourIssue","ReplicationTourIssue","Hots-
pot","Product","Context"]}}
```

> You can test that the Web Assistant redirect is working correctly by connecting to:
>
> ```
> https://webdispatcher:port/resources/sap/dfa/help/sap/
> cfg/XrayBootstrapHelpConfig.json
> ```
>
> If everything is OK, you will see a response of:
>
> ```
> {"description":"This configuration registers the
> Xray bootstrap plug-in", "modulePaths":{ "sap.dfa.
> help":"/resources/sap/dfa/help/~201509221536~"
> }, "bootstrapPlugins":{ "BootstrapXrayPlugin":{
> "module":"sap.dfa.help.utils.adapters.fiori.
> BootstrapXrayHelpPlugin"}}}}
> ```

Step 3: Install the Content Provider Certificate

You need to install the Content Provider server's SSL certificate on the Web Dispatcher so that it can establish a secure connection with SAP's Web Assistant server. Do this by carrying out the steps shown below.

1. Make sure you are logged on to your Web Dispatcher as an Administrator.

2. In the *Menu* on the left, select **WA1 | Monitor Application Servers**.

3. In the table on the right, click on the drop-down button in the **Name** column (this will be the entry for **Hostname** cp.hana.ondemand. com), and select **Establish Trust** from the drop-down menu. The *Certificate Wizard* is displayed.

4. Click on the **Import Certificate into SAPSSLC.pse** button in the **Actions** column for the **Issuer Certificate** record. The contents of the selected certificate are shown on the screen, as shown below.

5. Click **Import**.

6. The certificate will now be listed in the *Trusted Certificates* section of the *Web Dispatch Administration* screen.

You can test that Web Dispatcher is configured correctly by connecting to:

    https://webdispatcher:port/sap/public/icman/ping

where webdispatcher:port is the URL and port of your Web Dispatcher.

If everything is OK, you will see a response of:

    server on host xxxxxxx system xxxxxxx successfully
    reached

Setting up a Fiori Catalog and plugin

★ Consider creating two separate Catalogs, one with a plugin that has the parameter `editor=true` and one with a plugin that has `editor=false`. You can then create an Author role that uses the former ('true'), and a general user role that includes the latter ('false'). This will allow you to control who can access Edit Mode in the *Carousel* without relying on manual editing of the URL. See *Enabling the Editor* on page 59 for related information.

For S/4HANA on-premise systems (only) you need to set up a Fiori Catalog so that Web Assistant is accessible from the Launchpad, and then create a plugin for Web Assistant that you can assign to this.

Step 1: Create a Catalog

Create a new Fiori Catalog for Web Assistant by carrying out the steps shown below:

1. Access *Fiori Launchpad Designer*.

2. Click on the **Add** button at the bottom of the *Catalog Collection* panel on the left. The *Create Catalog* dialog box is displayed.

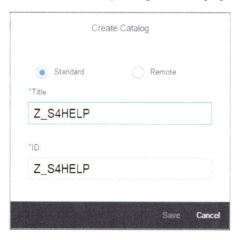

3. Enter a suitable name for the Catalog in the **Title** field, and a unique identifier into the **ID** field. These can be the same value.

4. Click **Save**. The Catalog is created, and listed in the *Catalog Collection* on the left of the screen.

Step 2: Create a plugin for the help system

1. Make sure your newly-created catalog is selected in the *Catalog Collection*, so its details (currently empty) are shown on the right.

2. In the rightmost section of the screen, select the **Target Mapping** tab, and then click on the **Create Target Mapping** button. The *Configure Catalog* screen is displayed.

3. In the **Semantic Object** field, enter **Shell**.

4. In the **Action** field, enter **plugin**.

5. In the **Application Type** field, select **SAPUI5 Fiori App** from the drop-down list

6. Enter any suitable name for the mapping in the **Title** field.

7. In the **URL** field, enter **/resources/sap/dfa/help/utils/adapters/fiori**.

8. In the **Component** field, enter **sap.dfa.help.utils.adapters.fiori**.

9. Enter a short description of the plugin in the **Information** field (you may want to mention "Web Assistant" or "Application Help" in this).

10. Under **Device Types**, select the **Desktop**, **Tablet**, and **Phone** checkboxes.

11. In the **Parameters** table at the bottom of the screen, enter the Name/Value pairs indicated in the table below. Note that some parameters are specific to the Content Scenario you are implementing.

● **Phone** is not recommended by the official documentation, but SAP added the **activatePhone** parameter for Web Assistant more recently, so perhaps this works, now.

● The version specified here is the version requested at display time, and shown in the *Help Context Information* dialog box (see the example on page 62).

| Scenario | | | PARAMETER | |
Standard	Custom	Extended	Name	Value
●	●	●	**product**	= *Your application name*
●	●	●	**version**	= *Your application version*
●			**serviceLayerVersion**	= **UACP**
	●			= **WPB**
		●		= **EXT**
●	●	●	**resourceUrl**	= **resources/sap/dfa/help**
			dataUrlUACP	= **https://help.sap.com/webassistant/**
			mediaUrlUACP	= **https://help.sap.com/doc/**
●		●	**dataUrlWPB**	= **https://cp.hana.ondemand.com**
	●			= *Your help content Workarea URL*
		●	**dataUrlWPB2**	= *Your help content Workarea URL*
-	-	-	**learningAppBackendUrl**	= *Your training content manager URL*
-	-	-	**learningAppWorkspace**	= *Your training content Workarea ID*

12. Enter any additional parameters you need to specify in the remaining rows in the **Parameters** table. If you need to enter more parameters than there are rows, click the **Add** button on the lower-right of the table, to add more rows.

For a list of all available parameters, refer to *Appendix A, Web Assistant Parameters*.

Step 3: Create a Mapping for consistent IDs

To improve consistent object recognition (which you need for hotspot assignment in the Web Assistant), you should create an additional target mapping. Do this as follows:

1. Within the same Catalog created earlier, click on the **Create Target Mapping** button again, to display a new instance of the *Configure Catalog* screen.

2. In the **Semantic Object** field, enter **Shell**.

3. In the **Action** field, enter **bootConfig**.

4. In the **Application Type** field, select **SAPUI5 Fiori App** from the drop-down list.

5. Enter any suitable name for the mapping (such as **Web Assistant Content Recognition Plugin**) in the **Title** field.

6. Leave the **URL** field blank.

7. Enter a suitable identifier (such as **Z_FLP_CONFIG**) in the **ID** field

8. In the **Parameters** table at the bottom of the screen, enter the following parameter:

   ◆ **Name**: **renderers/fiori2/componentData/config/enableHelp**
     Value: **true**

9. Save and close your Catalog definition.

Step 4: Create a Role

Once you have created a Fiori Catalog that is linked to the Web Assistant Framework and content, you need to create an SAP Authorization Role that will provide access to this Catalog—which in turn will make sure that your users can see the help content.

★ Consider creating two separate Catalogs— one with the parameter **editor=true** and one with **editor=false**. You can then create an Author role that uses the former, and a general user role that includes the latter.

To create a new role, work with your SAP Access team to carry out the following steps:

1. In Fiori, start transaction **PFCG**.

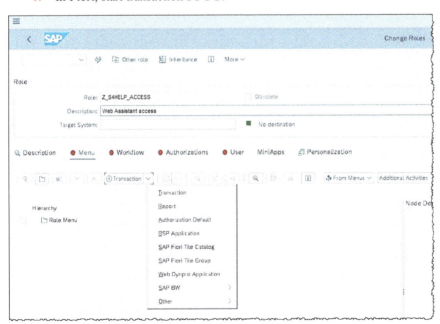

2. Enter a suitable name for the role (for example, **Z_S4HELP_ACCESS**) in the **Role** field

3. Enter a suitable description (for example, **Web Assistant access**) in the **Description** field.

4. Select the *Menu* tab, and then click on the **Role Menu** entry in the **Hierarchy** (this will be the only entry).

5. Select **SAP Fiori Tile Catalog** from the **Add** button drop-down. The *Assign Tile Catalog* dialog box is displayed.

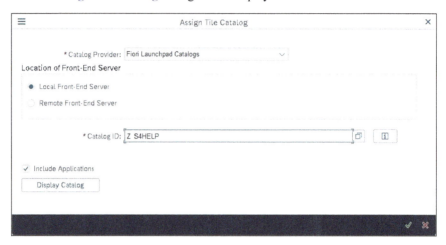

6. In the *Assign Tile Catalog* dialog box, perform the following actions:

   i.   In the **Catalog Provider** field, select **Fiori Launchpad Catalogs** from the drop-down list.

   ii. Under **Location of Front-End Server**, select **Local Front-End Server**.

   iii. In the **Catalog ID** field, enter or select the catalog you created previously (in our example above, this is **Z_S4HELP**).

   iv. Click **Continue**.

7. Back at the *Change Roles* screen, click on the *User* tab.

8. Assign the Role to all users. To achieve this, it is better to add this role to the default user access.

9. Set the validity date From today to 31st December 9999 (this grants access 'forever').

10. Click **Save**.

You have now finished the steps specific to on-premise S/4HANA. Continue with *Defining trusted sites in the browser* on page 54.

Define Communications for S/4HANA Cloud

Enabling Web Assistant for SAP S/4HANA Cloud edition or similar systems (including SAP Marketing Cloud, SAP Digital Manufacturing Cloud, and SAP Integrated Business Planning) requires specific configuration, as explained in this section. Note that this is only required if you want to create your own help content (Custom Content Scenario or Extended Content Scenario). If you only want to consume the SAP-provided help content (Standard Content Scenario), you do not need to do anything, and can skip this section (continue with *Defining trusted sites in the browser* on page 54).

Step 1: Create a new Communication System

The first step is to create a new Communication System in the application. This will connect the Web Assistant Content Provider (CP) to the application. Carry out the steps shown below.

1. Log into the application with administrator rights, and select the *Communication Management* group.

2. Click on the **Communication Systems** app.

3. Click **New**, at the bottom of the *Communication Systems* screen. The *New Communication System* dialog box is displayed.

4. Enter **ENABLE_NOW** into the **System ID** field.

5. Enter **ENABLE_NOW** into the **System Name** field.

6. Click **Create**. A new screen is displayed for the Communication System.

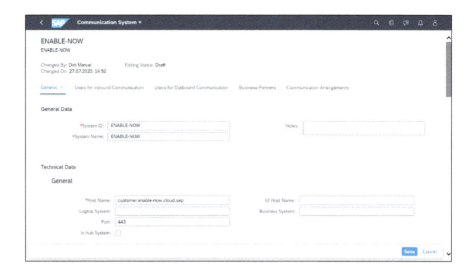

▲ Do not enter **https://** before the name, and do not enter a backslash on the end.

7. In the **Host Name** field, enter the domain name of your *Manager* (such as **globocorp.enable-now.cloud.sap**).

8. Enter **443** into the **HTTPS Port** field.

9. Click **Save**.

Step 2: Create a new Communication Arrangement

The second step is to create a Communication Arrangement. To do this, carry out the steps shown below.

1. Within the *Communication Management* group, click on the **Communication Arrangements** app.

2. Click **New**, at the bottom of the *Communication Arrangements* screen. The *New Communication Arrangements* dialog box is displayed.

3. In the **Scenario** field, select **SAP_COM_0011** from the drop-down list. The **Arrangement Name** will automatically be updated to specify the same thing.

4. Click **Create**. A new screen is displayed for the Communication Arrangement.

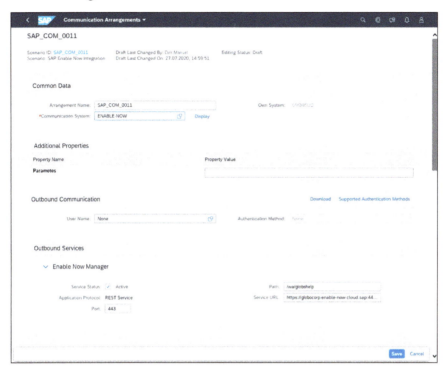

5. In the **Communication System** field, enter **ENABLE_NOW**. This is the identifier of the Communication System you created earlier.

6. Enter any Web Assistant parameters you need to specify in the **Parameters** field. Parameters should be separated by semicolons. Refer to *Appendix A, Web Assistant Parameters* for a full list of available parameters.

7. In the **Path** field, enter the path (on your *Manager*) of your help content Workarea.

   ♦ For a single-tenant implementation of SAP Enable Now, where your *Manager* URL is in the form
   `https://wpbxxxxxx.hana.ondemand.com`
   this path should be in the form **/wpb/wa/**{*Workarea_SID*}.

   ♦ For a multi-tenant implementation of SAP Enable Now, where your *Manager* URL is in the form
   `https://{customer}.enable-now.cloud.sap,`
   this path should be in the form **/wa/**{*Workarea_SID*}.

where *{Workarea_SID}* is the identifier of the Workarea in which your custom help content will be stored.

The **Service URL** field will automatically be populated based on the **Host Name** and **HTTPS Port** entered for the Communication System, and the **Path** specified here.

8. Click **Save**.

You have now finished the steps specific to S/4HANA Cloud. Continue with *Defining trusted sites in the browser* on page 54.

Creating a Cloud plugin

For applications on the SAP Cloud Platform (only), you need to create a new plugin app via the SCP Cockpit. Do this by carrying out the steps shown below.

1. In the cloud application, open the *SAP Cloud Platform Cockpit*.

2. Select **Services | Portal**.

3. Select **Go to Service**.

4. Select **Edit** for the *SAP Fiori Launchpad* site.

5. In the navigation pane on the left, expand **Content Management** and select **Apps**.

6. Click on the **New** (plus sign) button. The *New App* screen is displayed. Make sure the *Properties* page is selected.

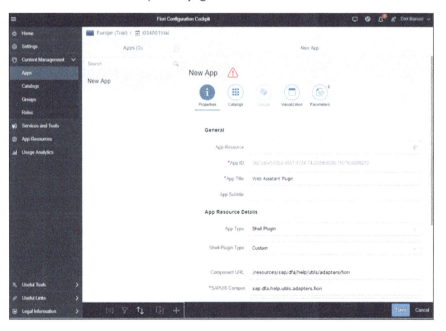

7. In the **App Title** field, enter a suitable name for the plugin (for example, "Web Assistant plugin").

8. Select an **App Type** of **Shell-plugin**.

9. Select a **Shell Plugin Type** of **Custom**.

10. In the **Component URL** field, enter **/resources/sap/dfa/help/utils/adapters/fiori**.

11. In the **SAPUI5 Component** field, enter **sap.dfa.help.utils.adapters.fiori**.

12. Click on the **Catalogs** button.

13. Select **Assign more catalogs**. The *Select Catalogs* dialog box is displayed.

14. Select a catalog and click on **Ok**.

15. Select the *Parameters* tab, then enter the following parameters:

Scenario			PARAMETER		
Standard	Custom	Extended	Name		Value
●	●	●	product	=	*Your application name*
●	●	●	version	=	*Your application version*
●			serviceLayerVersion	=	**UACP**
	●			=	**WPB**
		●		=	**EXT**
●		●	dataUrlWPB	=	**https://cp.hana.ondemand.com**
	●			=	*Your help content Workarea URL*
		●	dataUrlWPB2	=	*Your help content Workarea URL*

● The version specified here is the version requested at display time, and shown in the *Help Context Information* dialog box (see the example on page 62).

16. Enter any additional parameters you need to specify in the remaining rows in the **Parameters** table. For a list of all available parameters, refer to *Appendix A, Web Assistant Parameters*.

17. Click the **Save** button at the bottom of the screen to save your changes.

18. Click the **Publish** button, and then select **Publish** in the *Publish Site* dialog box.

You have now finished the steps specific to SAP Cloud Platform applications. Continue with *Defining trusted sites in the browser* on page 54.

Setting up SuccessFactors

★ There is rumor that all implementation scenarios will be simplified to the point where they closely resemble the SuccessFactors set-up, but this may be a few years off, as it requires customization of the target applications and not just SAP Enable Now.

Implementing Web Assistant for SuccessFactors is undoubtedly the easiest implementation scenario, consisting of a single screen on which all required settings can be made. Activate Web Assistant for Success Factors as follows:

1. In SuccessFactors, select **Admin Center**.

2. Enter "Web Assistant Settings" in the **Search** field, and then select **Web Assistant Settings** when this is shown in the drop-down list of search results. The following screen is displayed:

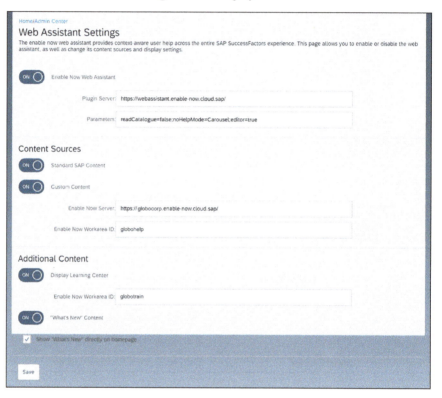

3. Set the **Enable Now Web Assistant** toggle button to **On**.

▲ Make sure you specify the **Plugin Server** URL exactly as noted here: with a back-slash at the end, and no space following it.

4. Enter **https://webassistant.enable-now.cloud.sap/** into the **Plugin Server** field. This is the location of the Web Assistant Framework, which provides the Web Assistant functionality.

5. Enter any required parameters you want to use for Web Assistant into the **Parameters** field. Parameters should be separated by semicolons. Refer to *Appendix A, Web Assistant Parameters* for a full list of available parameters.

6. If you want any available default (SAP-provided) content to be displayed in the *Carousel*, then set the **Standard SAP Content** toggle button to **On**, under *Content Sources*.

7. Complete the settings under *Custom Content* as follows:

♦ If you want *your own* (client-created) help content to be displayed in the *Carousel* (**EXT** or **WPB** modes), then use the following settings:

  i. Set the **Custom Content** toggle button to **On**.

  ii. Enter the URL of your SAP Enable Now installation into the **Enable Now Server** field.

  iii. Enter the ID (SID—not name!) of the Workarea in which your custom help content will be stored into the **Enable Now Workarea ID** field.

♦ If you want to see *only* the standard help content in the *Carousel* (**UACP** mode), then use the following settings:

  i. Set the **Custom Content** toggle button to **On** (even though this is not 'custom' content).

  ii. Enter **https://education.hana.ondemand.com/education/** into the **Enable Now Server** field.

  iii. Enter **sfsf** into the **Enable Now Workarea ID** field.

8. If you want the *Learning* page to be displayed in the *Carousel* (and remember that the only way to get to the *Learning Center* is via the *Learning* page) then set the **Display Learning Center** toggle button to **On** under *Additional Content*, and then complete the remaining field under *Display Learning Center* as follows:

♦ If you want *your own* (client-created) learning content to be displayed, then enter the identifier of the workarea from which the training content should be taken in the **Enable Now Workarea ID** field.

♦ If you want *only* the standard training content to be displayed, then enter **sfsf** in the **Enable Now Workarea ID** field.

9. If you want the *What's New* page to be available in the *Carousel* (assuming What's New content is available for the current application page at the time of display) then set the **"What's New" Content** toggle button to **On**.

10. If you have enabled the *What's New* page, and want the 'What's New message' (see *Displaying a What's New announcement* on page 94) to be displayed as soon as the user logs on to the application, then select the **Show "What's New" directly on homepage** checkbox.

11. Click **Save**. The message `Web Assistant Settings Saved Successfully` is displayed.

You have now finished the steps specific to on-premise S/4HANA. Continue with *Defining trusted sites in the browser* on page 54.

▲ Make sure the URL ends with a back-slash and there is no space following it.

● You do not need to specify an SAP Enable Now server here, as the same server specified under *Custom Content* is used.

■ If you want to be able to 'enhance' the standard content, you should specify your own Workarea here, but should define this as being based on the standard content Workarea (see *Extending a standard Workarea* on page 31).

Defining trusted sites in the browser

Most Web browsers will block or limit functionality for sites that it does not 'trust'. In order for Web Assistant to work correctly, the browser must have unfettered access to several specific websites that it needs. You should therefore add these required websites to the list of websites that it 'trusts'.

Often, companies will maintain a list of 'whitelisted' websites centrally, so that every user does not need to maintain them individually in their browser settings. You will likely need to contact the person or organization responsible for Internet security and ask them to perform the whitelisting for you.

Make sure the following sites are whitelisted:

- Your *Manager* URL, for example:
  - ♦ `https://globocorp.enable-now.cloud.sap`
  - ♦ `https://wpbxxxxxx.hana.ondemand.com`
- `https://{Your IAM}.accounts.ondemand.com` (If you are using SAP's IAM)
- `https://cp.hana.ondemand.com`
- `https://education.hana.ondemand.com`
- `https://xray.hana.ondemand.com`
- `https://accounts.sap.com`
- `https://webassistant.enable-now.cloud.sap`

You could also simplify things by just whitelisting `https://*.sap.com`, `https://*.cloud.sap`, and `https://*.ondemand.com` if your implementation allows this (you may have these whitelisted already if you are already running SuccessFactors or S/4HANA).

Enabling CORS

CORS stands for Cross-Origin Resource Sharing, and allows Web Assistant (running in one browser container ['origin']) to communicate with the application (running in another browser container). For Web Assistant, you need to set up CORS to allow interaction between the target application and your SAP Enable Now implementation.

■ You may notice a setting called **Enable Web Assistant** in this category. Ignore this. It enables Web Assistant help within Manager, and is not applicable to enabling Web Assistant for your applications.

Enable CORS on your SAP Enable Now server as follows:

1. Log on to *Manager*.

2. Select menu option **Administration | Server Settings**.

3. Locate the *Miscellaneous* category, and make the following changes:

- Enter * in the **CORS allowed sites** field. This will allow any other domain to communicate with your own SAP Enable Now *Manager*.

  If you need to need to provide tighter security, you can enter the specific domains you want to be able to cross-communicate. Typically this will include `*.cloud.sap`, `successfactors.com`, and so on.

- Select the **CORS enabled** checkbox.

4. Click **Save** to save your changes.

Additional Resources

Because implementing Web Assistant is a complex process that has many variables, you are encouraged to refer to the following additional resources which may provide additional help:

- *SAP Enable Now Web Assistant Integration Guide*

- *SAP Fiori: Setup and Configuration Guide*

- SAP Knowledge Base article **2823440** *SSO Configuration for Web Assistant*

- SAP Knowledge Base article **2715476** *Prerequsites for SSO Configuration of SAP Enable Now*

You can find the guides on the Info Center (`enable-now.sap.com`). The Knowledge Base articles can be located via the SAP Support site (`support.sap.com`).

Summary

Getting Web Assistant up and running is a lengthy and sometimes confusing process. This is largely because there are so many variables, including the target application and the system topology (including authentication methods). Some integration steps may be complete already, or may need to be executed by other personnel within the company or organization.

Regardless of the specific scenario under which Web Assistant is being implemented, SAP Enable Now Authors will need to decide upon a content delivery scenario (Standard, Custom, or Extended), and will need to organize their Workareas appropriately, to support this.

3

Creating Help Content

In this chapter, we will look at how to create help content that appears in the *Carousel*, directly from within Web Assistant. This requires you to have write permission to the linked Workarea.

In this chapter, you will learn:

- How to create a Help Tile
- How to create a Link Tile
- How to create a Guided Tour
- How to create What's New content

Deciding what to create

Before jumping right in to creating your help content, you should take a minute to consider exactly what you want to create. Web Assistant allows you to provide field-level context help and Guided Tours; it allows you to provide access to other SAP Enable Now courseware (including Books, Book Pages, and Simulations); and it allows you to link to other, external sources of information such as an existing knowledge repository. Knowing which of these to provide—and when—is more important than just knowing how to create Help Tiles.

First, take an inventory of any existing help or training material. Perhaps it is sufficient to provide access to this material from Link Tiles on the relevant application pages.

> If you do link to existing content, make sure the linked content is specific to the application page from which you are linking it—there is no point in having context-sensitive Link Tiles on 50 application pages that all point to

the same PDF User Guide that the user then has to wade through to find the relevant section.

Also check for any existing SAP Enable Now courseware for the same application. For example, if you already have a Simulation that provides step-by-step instructions for a task, do you really need to provide a Guided Tour as well? Certainly an in-application Guided Tour would be a better solution, but if you are constrained on time and/or budget you may be better off just providing access to the Simulation via from *Learning* page. You can then put your efforts into providing a few specific Help Tiles to augment this.

If you do have existing content (SAP Enable Now courseware or external content) but replace this with Web Assistant help, make sure you go back and remove the old content once the Web Assistant help is in place—and provide change communications (and redirects) where appropriate.

If you do not have any existing content that you can leverage (or you want to replace it to provide a better EPSS through Web Assistant), consider whether Guided Tours are the correct solution. Quite often they will be, but do you need a Guided Tour for every business task? You might want to only provide full Guided Tours for only the most commonly-performed tasks—working on the assumption that these will be referred to most often. Or you may decide to provide Guided Tours only for infrequently-performed tasks—working on the assumption that this is where users are most likely to need a 'reminder'.

Even within a Guided Tour, think about whether you need full step-by-step help for every field the user has to complete. Maybe the application interface is fairly intuitive and most of the fields are self-explanatory. If this is the case, instead of providing Hotspot-tethered Tour steps of (for example) "Enter the customer's phone number in the Phone field.", "Enter the customer's fax number into the Fax field." and so on, perhaps you just need a single, un-tethered Step of "Enter the customer's contact details in the Communication section.".

Perhaps you just need a few Help Tiles for the 'less-obvious' fields, or fields with specific requirements. For example, if all fields are self-explanatory apart from one, where you have an in-house naming convention, perhaps you only need to provide a Help Tile for this specific field. Again, don't feel that you need to provide a Help Tile for *every* field, just because you can. If the majority of your Help Tiles aren't perceived to be adding value, your users will stop referring to *any* of the Help Tiles. By contrast, if there are only Hotspots for a few selected fields (those for which you need to provide important information) users are much more likely to click on them and see your help information.

Finally, bear in mind that every tethered Help Tile will have a visible Hotspot on the screen (whether this is a circle, rectangle, underline, or icon), and an overabundance of these can 'clutter' the screen. You do not want to overwhelm your users—you are there to help them.

There is a reason why the *Help Topics* page is the first one displayed when a user opens the *Carousel*. This should provide the users with *immediate* help. If they need more detailed help, they can progress to the *Guided Tours* page. And if that doesn't help, they can go to the *Learning* page, where they can access the full training. It is a graduated approach, where users start at the most detailed level, and broaden their search until they find the help they are looking for. Build your EPSS to support this.

Enabling the Editor

To create help content, the *Carousel* needs to be displayed, and you have to be in Edit Mode. Unlike the *Producer* and *Manager*, the *Carousel Editor* is not automatically available to you just because you have the correct permissions. Instead, it must be 'enabled', via the **editor** parameter. In a non-Production system, this parameter can be entered in the configuration for the target application, but you should not do this for your Production system. For Production systems, it is usually left up to the Authors to manually add this parameter to the URL, as follows:

```
&help-editor=true
```

Once the *Editor* has been enabled, you will see a few additional buttons at the bottom of the *Carousel Help Stripe*: These are:

Icon	Name	Description
✕	**Close**	Close the Web Assistant *Carousel* (including the *Help Stripe*).
🌐	**Toggle Editor / Published Stage**	Toggle between showing only published content in the *Carousel* and displaying draft (unpublished) content as well.
✏	**Enter / Exit Edit Mode**	Enter or exit Edit Mode. When you are in Edit Mode, the button is 'highlighted'.
»	**Minimize**	Hide the *Carousel* 'content bar', leaving only the *Help Stripe* displayed.

The Carousel Editor

To access the *Carousel Editor*, click on the **Edit** button on the *Help Stripe*.

Edit

If no help content exists for the current application context, then the following dialog box is displayed:

■ If you have separate Development and Production application systems and they both point to the same SAP Enable Now Workarea, you can choose to enable the *Editor* by default in the (restricted access) Development system, but not in the Production system.

● The **Close** button is only displayed if the parameter **showCloseButton=true** is specified.

▲ It is important to understand that if the *Editor* is enabled, the **Edit** button will still be displayed—and work— even if you do not have edit permissions on the connected Workarea. You just won't be able to save any changes you make. So check your permissions before you start any work.

● The **Minimize** button can be suppressed by specifying the parameter **showMinimizeButton =false**.

★ You can prevent your users from seeing this dialog box by specifying the parameter noHelpMode with a value of anything other than nothing.

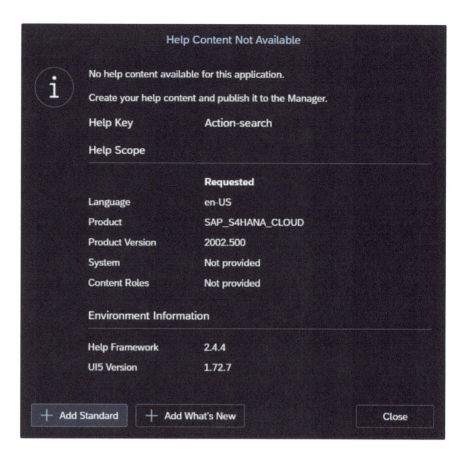

● If you compare the information in this dialog box with the example on page 62 you'll see what the problem is: there is no **Available** information here.

This simply indicates that no Help Project exists for the current application page (shown in the **Help Key**). Here, your options are:

- Click **Add Standard** to add a *Help Content* page to the *Carousel*. This will be empty until you add some content to it.

- Click **Add What's New** to add a *What's New* page to the *Carousel*. Again, this will be empty until you add some content to it.

- Click **Close** to exit from Edit Mode. The *Learning* page (if enabled) will be the only page available in the *Carousel*.

The Editor Help Stripe

When you are in Edit Mode, the *Help Stripe* is expanded to include the following additional buttons:

Icon	Name	Description
+	Add Help Topic	Add help content (Guided Tour, Help Tile, Link Tile, or What's New content).

Icon	Name	Description
	Save Changes	Save your changes to the server.
	Undo	Undo the last change you made.
	Hide Hotspots	Toggle between hiding and showing any Hotspots on the current screen (in Edit Mode only—this will not affect what users see). This is useful if the Hotspots are 'getting in the way' of elements you need to see while you are editing.
	Options	This button provides access to a number of important features—see *The Options button*, below.

The Options button

The **Options** button is displayed when you are in Edit Mode. Clicking on this button displays a pop-up menu similar to the one shown below:

Show Context Information...

Show Keyboard Shortcuts...

Show in Manager Workspace...

Edit in Manager Web-Editor...

Publish Help

Remove Help

Product Feedback

Release Information...

Note that the options available in the pop-up menu will depend upon the *Carousel* page that is currently displayed. This example is taken from the *Help Topics* page. We'll look at the content type specific options as we create each content type later in this chapter. For now, let's look at the common options.

Show Context Information

Select this option to display context information for the current application page.

■ You can press
CTRL+SHIFT+I at any time
(even in Display Mode) to
display this dialog box.

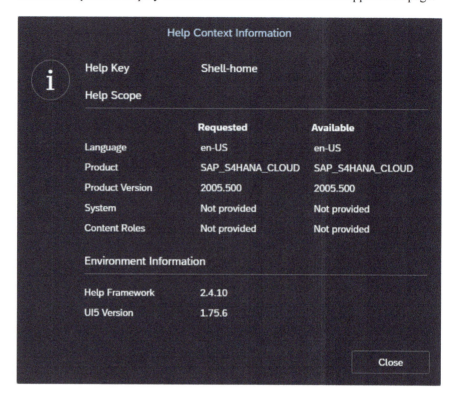

The key information to note in this dialog box is:

- **Help Key**: The identifier of the current application page. For Help Tiles, this is used as the name of the Help Project.

- **Requested**: The context information of the current page.

- **Available**: The context information of the help content retrieved from the Workarea (and displayed in the *Carousel*).

- **Help Framework**: The version number of Web Assistant.

■ Generally, you would
expect the **Requested** and
Available values to be the
same if help is displayed.
The only time they would
not be is if help was
requested for a specific
language but this is not
available so the fallback
English version is provided
instead.

The context information provided is useful for troubleshooting (for example, when trying to determine why your content is not being displayed for the application page as expected), but you will also need it when 'contextualizing' non-help content, as explained in *Contextualizing a learning content object* on page 153.

Keyboard Shortcuts

Select this option to display a cheat-sheet of keyboard shortcuts you can use when creating and editing your help content. The graphic below shows the shortcuts valid at the time of writing, although new ones are added from time-to-time.

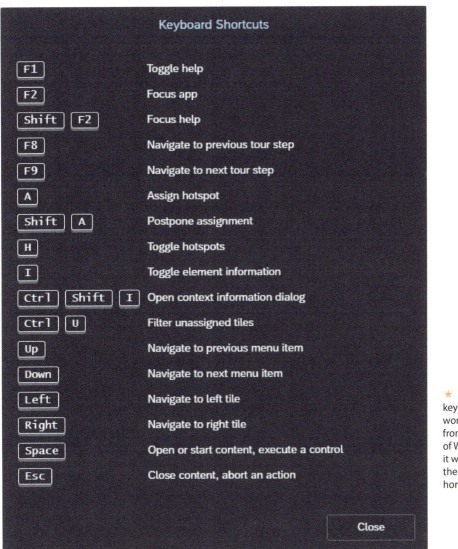

Keyboard Shortcuts

F1		Toggle help
F2		Focus app
Shift	F2	Focus help
F8		Navigate to previous tour step
F9		Navigate to next tour step
A		Assign hotspot
Shift	A	Postpone assignment
H		Toggle hotspots
I		Toggle element information
Ctrl	Shift	I	Open context information dialog
Ctrl	U	Filter unassigned tiles
Up		Navigate to previous menu item
Down		Navigate to next menu item
Left		Navigate to left tile
Right		Navigate to right tile
Space		Open or start content, execute a control
Esc		Close content, abort an action

Close

★ The *Left* and *Right* keyboard shortcuts do not work; they are left over from a previous version of Web Assistant in which it was possible to have the *Carousel* displayed horizontally.

Show in Manager Workspace

Help content is saved to your Workarea in 'Projects'. Each Guided Tour is saved in a separate Project, but all Help Tiles and Link Tiles for a single application page are saved together in a single Project. What's New content is also saved to its own Project (per application page).

Selecting the **Show In Manager Workspace** menu option opens *Manager* in a separate browser tab, and positions you on the Project for the current help content object. This is extremely useful for finding your help content objects, because as noted earlier all help content Projects are initially stored in the **Unsorted** Group of your Workarea. To make things worse, Help Tile Projects use the **Help Key** (identifier) of the application page as the Project name, which can make them difficult to locate, if you are not familiar with these.

Edit in Manager Web-Editor

Selecting this option opens the current Help Project in the *Web Editor*. Although you will typically perform most of your editing directly in the *Carousel* (as explained in this chapter), there are additional things you can do in the *Web Editor* that you cannot do in the *Carousel Editor* (such as inserting tables, images, or videos). These things are explained in *Chapter 4, Using the Web Editor*.

Product Feedback

This option directs you to a simple survey form where you can provide some generic feedback on the SAP Enable Now product. It is not specific to Web Assistant (although here is the only place in the entire SAP Enable Now product that this feedback option appears), and there is no option to provide 'free-form' comments. This feedback is sent directly to SAP.

Release Information

+ The **Release Information** option was added in Version 2.3.12.

This option provides access to the *What's New* document for each release of SAP Enable Now (and not just the current release), via the *Info Center*. You will find it helpful to check this page periodically. Minor versions can be released every few weeks, and may not always be fully communicated via the channels you monitor.

Publish Help or Publish Tour

This option will be listed as **Publish Help** for the *Help Topics* and *What's New* pages, and **Publish Tour** for a Guided Tour. You use it to publish the help content currently displayed on the *Carousel*. For the *Help Topics* page, this will publish *all* of the Help Tiles and Link Tiles for the current application page (it is not possible to publish only selected Help Tiles). For Guided Tours, this will publish only the currently-displayed Guided Tour.

Note that if there are unpublished changes on the current screen, then the **Status** icon in the *Carousel* will be yellow. You can save and exit without publishing, but users will not see your changes until you publish them.

Status (Draft)

Publishing content is covered in *Publishing Help Content* on page 96.

Providing content on the Help Topics page

As explained in *Chapter 1, An Introduction to Web Assistant*, the *Help Topics* page can contain Help Tiles and Link Tiles. These look the same in the *Carousel*, but are created differently, so we'll look at them separately.

Creating a Help Tile

A Help Tile is a single Tile on the *Carousel* that can display a single 'Bubble' of help content. This Bubble may or may not be associated with a specific element (such as an input field or a button) on the screen.

To create a Help Tile, carry out the steps shown below.

1. In the application, navigate to the page for which you want to provide a Help Tile.

2. Click on the **Open Help** button. The *Carousel* is displayed.

3. Make sure you are on the *Help Topics* page within the *Carousel*.

4. Click on the **Edit** button, to switch into Edit Mode. (When you are in Edit Mode the button appears 'selected' [highlighted].)

Edit

5. Click on the **Add** button. A pop-up menu is shown, providing you with a number of options for things you can add to the *Carousel*.

Add

■ Even though you are on the *Help Topics* page, you will see options to add a Guided Tour or What's New content. Selecting either of these automatically switches the *Carousel* to the appropriate page.

6. Select **Add Help Tile**. The *Edit Content* dialog box is displayed.

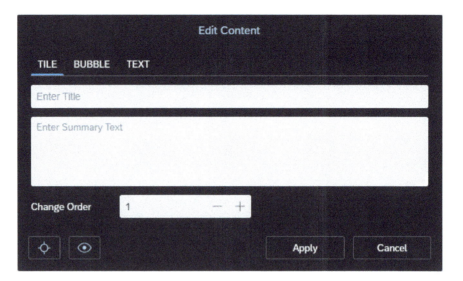

7. On the *Tile* tabbed page, enter a short title for the Help Tile into the **Tile Title** ("Enter title") field. Limit this to one (very short) line. As a tip, consider using the name of the screen element to which the Help Tile relates.

8. In the **Tile Text** ("Enter Summary Text") field, enter the additional text that should appear in the Tile, below the title. You should limit this to a single, short sentence if possible, because Tiles will display a maximum of four (*Carousel*-width) lines of **Tile Text**.

9. By default, this new Help Tile will be inserted after any existing Help Tiles on the *Carousel*. If you want the Tile to appear in a specific sequence, then use the **Change Order** field to enter or select the sequential position where you want it to appear.

10. Click the **Bubble** tab.

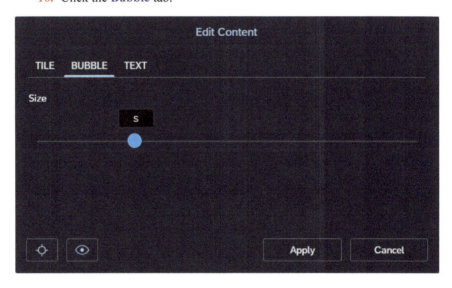

11. You can manually adjust the dimensions of the bubble that will be displayed for this Help Tile by dragging the **Bubble Size** slider to **XS**, **S**, **M**, **L**, or **XL** as necessary. This is optional, as Bubbles are always automatically sized to accommodate the **Bubble Text** entered on the *Text* tabbed page. This setting defines the relative *width* of the Bubble, so a value of **XL** will result in a very wide but relatively short Bubble, and a value of **XS** will result in a relatively narrow but taller Bubble. These are 'relative' sizes (the values do not equate to an absolute number of pixels) so you may need to play around to find the size that works best for this particular Bubble.

12. Click on the **Text** tab.

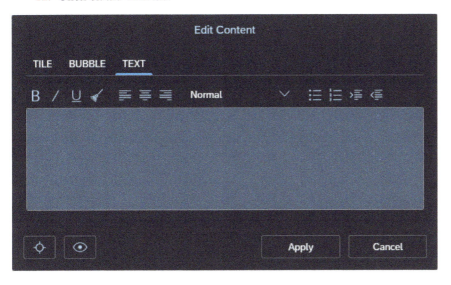

13. In the **Bubble Text** (text area) field, enter the text that you want to appear in the Bubble for this Help Tile. You can enter practically any amount of text in this field, but be careful not to overwhelm the user. If you have a lot of information to provide, consider placing (most of) it in a linked Book Page.

The buttons above the text area provide you with some basic text formatting features. These are likely to be familiar to most Authors, but for the sake of completeness they are listed in the table below.

Button	Name	Purpose
B	Bold	Set the currently-selected text to bold.
I	Italics	Set the currently-selected text to italics.
U	Underline	Underline the currently-selected text. This is not recommended as it can be confused for a hyperlink.

Button	Name	Purpose
	Remove Formatting	Remove any direct formatting applied to the selected text.
	Align Left	Left-align the current paragraph.
	Align Center	Center the current paragraph.
	Align Right	Right-align the current paragraph.
	Style Selector	Use the drop-down to select a pre-built paragraph style to apply to the currently-selected paragraph(s).
	Bullets	Format the currently-selected paragraph(s) as a bulleted list.
	Numbering	Format the currently-selected paragraph(s) as a numbered list.
	Indent	Indent the currently-selected paragraph(s).
	Outdent	Remove one level of indentation from the currently-selected paragraph.

Further options for the **Bubble Text** are available in the *Web Editor*. This includes font formatting options, and the ability to insert tables, images, and video. Full details can be found in *Using the Text Editor* on page 109.

■ You can always assign Hotspots later. In Edit Mode, you can press *Ctrl+U* on the keyboard to filter the *Carousel* to show only Help Tiles that do not have a Hotspot assigned to them, to make completing the help easier.

At this stage, the Help Tile has not been assigned to an element on the screen. If you do *not* want the Help Tile to be tied to a specific screen element, then you can jump ahead to Step 18. Otherwise, continue with Step 14.

14. Click on the **Assign Hotspot** button in the lower-left corner of the *Edit Content* dialog box.

Assign Hotspot

15. The *Edit Content* dialog box is hidden, and the cursor changes to a cross-hairs. Move the cursor over the element on the application screen to which this Help Tile should be connected.

As you hover over different elements on the screen, a colored border is shown around the element, and a 'recognition indicator' (of the same color) is shown below the element. This indicates the suitability of the element for use as the target of a Hotspot. Suitability is determined by whether the element can be uniquely and consistently identified on the application page. This is critical to the ability of the Web Assistant to provide context-sensitive help. The table below shows the different types of recognition indicators that may be shown, and explains how these relate to the suitability of the element for consistent recognition.

Recognition Indicator	Suitability
Element: A	The element is identified by an attribute implemented specifically for SAP Enable Now's use. This is perfect for Hotspot assignment.
Element: INPUT	The element is identified by a unique attribute within the user interface (UI) design which is likely stable and consistent. Hotspot assignment is probably reliable.
⚑ Element: A	The element cannot be identified by a stable attribute, but its name is consistent so is being used. This name may be language-dependent, so Hotspot assignment may need to be recaptured on localized versions.
Element: A	The element does not have any reliable attributes, which makes it unsuitable for Hotspot assignment. You can still use it, but its identification for context help will likely be unreliable.

Even when you have identified the element you think you want to use, you should move the cross-hair cursor around slightly to make sure you are selecting the most suitable element. This is because some elements may be nested within other elements. To help you with this, the element type is displayed immediately below the identified element area, as shown in the examples above.

As an additional check that you are selecting a suitable screen element, you can press the *I* key on the keyboard (during Hotspot assignment) to display the *Recognition Information* panel at the bottom of the screen. You should not *need* to refer to this information (or the explanation below) but it can be useful for troubleshooting. An example of this panel is shown below:

Recognition Rule:	DataAttrSelector
Element Tag / Element ID:	LI / __item0-anchorNavigationBar-1
Element Offset:	x: 0.7355, y: 0.7083
Element Selector:	LI[data-help-id='id-1590023523321-16']

● Once you select an element for Hotspot assignment, the **Recognition Rule** and **Element Selector** are stored on the *Element* tabbed page of the *Edit Content* dialog box (this tab is only available once the Hotspot has been assigned).

The **Recognition Rule** indicates how Web Assistant has identified the element. The list below shows the possible values of the Recognition Rule. For the technically-minded, it also explains where you can find the details of the matched element in each case. The list shows the values in order of suitability—which is the same order in which the four Recognition Indicators are listed in the table above.

1. **DataAttrSelector**: The identifier of the element used is shown in the **Element Selector**, as the value of the **data-help-id** parameter

2. **IDSelectorUI5**: The identifier used is shown as the **Element ID**

3. **TextSelector**: The identifier used is shown as the **Element ID**

4. **DomSelectorUI5**: The identifier used is shown in the **Element Selector**, as the value of the **id$** parameter

Always use the element that is identified using the most reliable Recognition Rule available. This will provide the best chance of the context-sensitive help being consistently displayed in the correct position on the screen (that is, pointing to this exact element—even if the size of the screen or the location of this element changes).

If the element *cannot* be consistently identified, you can still assign the Hotspot to it, but should bear in mind that during playback the Help Bubble may not be positioned as accurately as it would otherwise be (it will still be displayed, but may not point to the exact element—or, indeed, to any element). Alternatively, consider not assigning a Hotspot at all, and just having the Bubble displayed in the center of the screen. If you do this, consider including an image of the element in the Bubble, to help users identify the element themselves.

⭐ If you are not ready to click on the target object, use the keyboard shortcut *SHIFT+A* to 'defer' hotspot selection until after the next mouse-click. This is useful if you need to perform some action to make the target object visible—for example, for objects on drop-down lists.

➕ The *Element* tabbed page was introduced in Version 2.3.12. It contains technical information relating to the hotspot, and does not need to be changed.

➕ The **Preview** button was added to the *Edit Content* dialog box in Version 2.3.12.

■ If you subsequently decide that you do not want the help content to be associated with a specific object, you can return to the *Actions* pop-up menu for the Help Tile or Guided Tour Step and select **Center on Screen**, to center the Bubble on the screen.

16. Once you have identified the appropriate element for the Hotspot, click on it to select it.

17. When you click on the element, the *Edit Content* dialog box is re-displayed. This will now have two additional tabs: *Hotspot* and *Element*. Select the **Hotspot** tab. The contents of the *Hotspot* page will depend upon the value selected in the **Hotspot Style** field, which specifies the way in which the Hotspot should appear in the application. Refer to the relevant *Hotspot Style* section below for details on how to complete the available fields, and then continue with Step 18. (If you're impatient to see some results then just leave this tab as-is and go straight to Step 18—you can always come back and change things later.)

Tip:

If you want to see how your Help Bubble will look before you commit your changes (by clicking **Apply** in the next step), you can click on the **Preview** button. This is useful for confirming that the Highlight position and bubble position are correct, before saving.

Preview

18. Once you have specified all of the Help Tile details, click **Apply**. The *Edit Content* dialog box is closed and your new Help Tile is visible in the *Carousel*. If you assigned a Hotspot then a 'Hotspot' icon is shown in the upper-left corner of the Help Tile to indicate that it has been assigned to a screen element.

19. Click on the **Save Changes** button on the *Help Stripe* to save your changes.

20. Click on the **Edit Mode** button to exit from Edit Mode.

Save Changes

Don't forget you still need to publish your Help Tile (as explained in *Publishing Help Content* on page 96). It will only be visible in draft mode until you do so.

Hotspot Style: Circle

If you select a **Hotspot Style** of **Circle** (which is the default selection), then the Hotspot is identified by a circle, which (by default) is overlaid onto the screen element, as shown below:

Prior to Version 2.3.10, **Circle** was the only style available.

If the user clicks on the circle, the associated Help Bubble is displayed. Note that because the Hotspot is clickable, you should always make sure that its size and position do not prevent the user from interacting with the element underneath it if they need to.

An example of the *Edit Content* dialog box when the **Hotspot Style** is set to **Circle** is shown below.

Define the Hotspot details in the available fields, as follows:

1. Make sure the **Hotspot Style** field specifies **Circle**.

2. If you want the circle to be centered on the exact point on the element where you clicked, then select the **Use Click Position** checkbox. Otherwise, deselect this checkbox and the circle will be centered on the middle point of the element (but see the **Offset** fields).

3. If you selected the **Use Click Position** checkbox, then the **Position** fields indicate exactly where in the element you clicked. The circle will be centered on this point. You can move the location of this point by changing these fields.

   Using Position fields
   The field on the left specifies the percentage of the way along the horizontal (X) axis (in from the leftmost edge of the element) and the field on the right specifies the percentage of the way down the vertical (Y) axis (down from the top edge of the element). To change the these values, either over-type the fields with new values, or use the plus/minus icons to increase/decrease the values (by 5% at a time, and rounded up to the nearest 1%).

➕ The **Offset** fields were added in Version 2.3.10.

4. If necessary, you can move the center-point of the circle (regardless of whether or not you are using the click-position) a specific number of pixels (in any direction) by adjusting the **Offset** fields as necessary.

   Using Offset fields
   The first **Offset** field specifies the number of pixels to offset the point on the X axis (a negative number will move the reference point to the left; a positive number will move it to the right). The second **Offset** field specifies the number of pixels to offset the point on the Y axis (a negative number will move the reference point up; a positive number will move it down). To change these values, either over-type the fields with new values, or use the plus/minus icons to increase/decrease the values (one pixel at a time).

■ Consistency is (always) important. You should strive to use the same size circles across all your help content, where possible. Different sizes could be interpreted by your users as implying different levels of importance. The Master Author should specify a default size in the Style Guide.

5. You can adjust the size of the circle by dragging the **Size** slider to **XS**, **S**, **M**, **L**, or **XL**.

Hotspot Style: Rectangle

If you select a **Hotspot Style** of **Rectangle**, then the Hotspot is identified by a rectangular border, which (by default) is drawn around the perimeter of the selected element, as shown below:

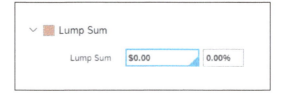

The lower-right corner of the rectangle is a triangular tab that the user can click to display the associated Help Bubble. This means that the user does not click on the rectangle itself, and can therefore interact with the element within it if necessary.

An example of the *Edit Content* dialog box when the **Hotspot Style** is set to **Rectangle** is shown below:

There is only one pair of fields available for a rectangle. These are the **Change Size** fields, which you can use to increase or decrease the width and/or height of the Rectangle (for example, to increase the space between the rectangle and the element). You can either over-type the fields with new values, or use the plus/minus icons to increase/decrease the values (one pixel at a time). Note that the rectangle will always be centered on the element; you cannot change this.

■ Use even numbers to 'balance' the space around the object.

Hotspot Style: Underline

If you select a **Hotspot Style** of **Underline**, the Hotspot is identified by a single line drawn underneath the screen element, as shown below:

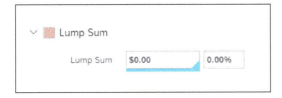

As with the rectangle, there is a triangular 'tab' on the right that the user clicks on to display the associated Help Bubble.

An example of the *Edit Content* dialog box when the **Hotspot Style** is set to **Underline** is shown below.

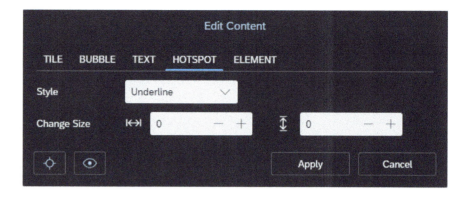

As with the **Rectangle**, there is only one pair of fields available here. Again, these are the **Change Size** fields, but here they have a slightly different purpose. The field on the left is still used to control the width of the underline (which is horizontally centered on the element), but the field on the right is used to move the underline up or down relative to the bottom edge of the screen element. As before, you can either over-type the fields with new values, or use the plus/minus icons to increase/decrease the values, one pixel at a time.

Hotspot: Icon

If you select a **Hotspot Style** of **Icon**, a small image (icon) is displayed close to the element. There are a lot of options available for the type and position of the icon, but here's an example of what it would typically look like:

The user can click on the icon to display the associated Help Bubble.

Here is an example of the *Edit Content* dialog box when the **Hotspot Style** is set to **Icon**.

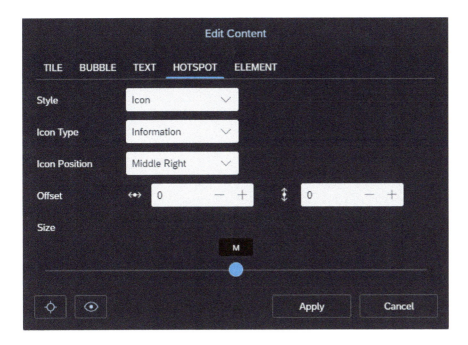

Define the details of the icon Hotspot in the available fields, as follows:

1. Make sure the **Hotspot Style** field specifies **Icon**.

2. Select the icon to use from the **Icon Type** drop-down. As of the date of publishing of this book, the following options are available:

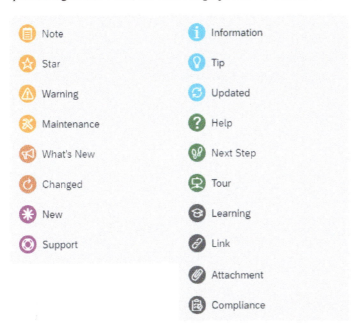

The **Note**, **Maintenance**, **Tip**, and **Compliance** icons were added in Web Assistant Version 2.4.8.

3. Select the position of the icon relative to the screen element from the **Icon Position** drop-down. The following options are available (the image on the left of each option shows the approximate position of the icon [the dot] relative to the screen element [the square]):

	Manual	·□	Middle Left
⊡	Centered	□·	Middle Right
˙□	Top Left, Outside	.□	Bottom Left
ḃ	Top Left, Above	□.	Bottom Right
ḋ	Top Center	,□	Bottom Left, Outside
ď	Top Right, Above	ᑫ	Bottom Left, Below
□˙	Top Right, Outside	ᑫ	Bottom Center
˙□	Top Left	ᑫ	Bottom Right, Below
□˙	Top Right	□,	Bottom Right, Outside

If you choose **Manual** then the icon will be centered on the element, and you will probably need to use the **Offset** fields (below) to adjust the position of the icon relative to the element.

4. If necessary, you can use the **Offset** fields to adjust the absolute position of the Icon relative to the position set by the **Icon Position** field. You can either over-type the fields with new values, or use the plus/minus icons to increase/decrease the values (one pixel at a time). Refer to the note *Using Offset fields* on page 72 for additional instructions, if necessary.

5. You can adjust the size of the icon by dragging the **Size** slider to **XS**, **S**, **M**, **L**, or **XL**. Again, consistency across your help system is important, so try to use the same size for all Hotspots.

Creating a Link Tile

In earlier releases, it was possible to assign a Hotspot to a Link Tile. This is no longer the case.

A Link Tile is very similar to a Help Tile, but instead of the Tile providing a Bubble that contains (typically) text, clicking on a Link Tile displays a linked object instead. This object can be a Book or Book Page, a non-Enable Now file that you imported into your Workarea (such as a PDF file or video), or even an external website. This is a good way of providing additional information to your users.

To create a Link Tile carry out the steps shown below.

1. In the application, navigate to the page for which you want to provide a Link Tile.

2. Click on the **Open Help** button. The *Carousel* is displayed.

3. Click on the **Edit** button, to switch into Edit Mode. (When you are in Edit Mode the button appears 'selected' [highlighted].)

Edit

4. Click on the **Add** button, and select **Add Link Tile** from the drop-down menu. The *Edit Content* dialog box is displayed.

Add

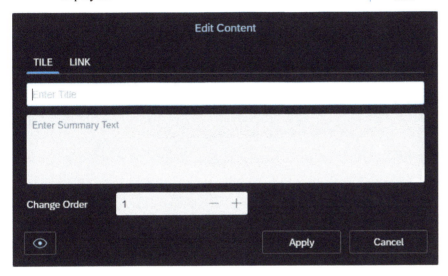

5. In the **Tile Title** ("Enter Title") field, enter a short title for the Tile. This should be short enough to fit on one line of a Tile on the *Carousel*.

6. In the **Tile Text** ("Enter Summary Text") field, enter a slightly longer text that explains the purpose of the tile. This should be no longer than can fit in a single Tile. You may find it useful to explain what document or other object will be displayed if the user clicks on the Tile.

7. By default, this new Link Tile will be inserted after any existing Help Tiles on the *Carousel*. If you want the Tile to appear in a specific position within the existing tiles, then enter or select the sequential position where you want it to appear in the **Change Order** field.

8. Click on the **Link** tab. The *Link* tabbed page is displayed, as shown below.

● This example shows all possible fields for the *Link* page. In reality, the **Lightbox Sizing** and **Show as Announcement** fields are only displayed if you select the **Open in Lightbox** option, the **Lightbox Size** fields are only displayed if you select a **Lightbox Sizing** of **User-Defined** or **User-Defined (Overlay)**, and the **Occurrences** field is only displayed if you select **Show as Announcement**.

● If you are linking to an Enable Now content in the same Workarea, you can leave the **Link to** field blank for now, and use the *Web Editor* (as explained in *Chapter 4, Using the Web Editor*) where you can navigate to and select the content object via the **Link To** property.

▲ You should only link to an external resource if you have a high degree of confidence it will continue to be available at the specified location. Where possible, linked content should reside within your Workarea, where you can control it.

9. In the **Link to** ("Enter URL") field, enter (or paste) the URL of the object, document, or web page that should be displayed when the user clicks on the Tile. If you are linking to a content object in Enable Now, then you should use the URL provided in the object's **Published View** or **Custom View** property (in the *Start Links* category—see *Obtaining links to training content* on page 166).

> ## Tips for linking external files
>
> For PDFs, you can link to a specific page within the document by appending #page=n to the URL.
>
> For YouTube videos:
>
> - Make sure you use the 'embeddable' link (by selecting **Embed** in the *Share* dialog box), and then copying the URL from the `iframe` code (not the whole `iframe`—just the URL within double-quotes on the `src` statement, which will contain `/embed`).
> - Add the parameter **autoplay=1** to start playback automatically.
> - Add the parameter **rel=0** to suggest only 'related videos' from the same channel when your embedded video finishes.

■ A lightbox works well for any content that can be embedded in an HTML iFrame.

10. By default, the linked object will be opened in a new browser window. If you want it to be opened in a 'lightbox' (an overlay on top of the application page), then complete the following fields:

i.   Select the **Open in Lightbox** checkbox.

ii. Use the **Lightbox Sizing** slider to select the option that controls the way in which the lightbox will be sized. The following options are available:

- ♦ **Full**: The lightbox will be displayed as large as possible, within the entire browser window.

- ♦ **Client**: The lightbox will be displayed as large as possible within the client (application) area of the screen (that is, excluding the *Carousel*, so the *Carousel* remains visible). Note that if the object is larger than can fit within just the client area, it will extend over the *Carousel* anyway.

- ♦ **User-Defined**: The lightbox will be displayed centered within the client (application) area of the screen (that is, excluding the *Carousel*, and at the size specified in the **Lightbox Sizing** fields (see below).

- ♦ **User-Defined (Overlay)**: The lightbox will be displayed centered on the entire browser window, and at the size specified in the **Lightbox Sizing** fields (see below)—even if this overlaps the *Carousel*.

iii. If you selected a **Lightbox Sizing** of **User-Defined** or **User-Defined (Overlay)** then use the **Lightbox Size** fields to specify the width and height of the lightbox, in pixels. If you are linking to a Book Page, and Book Pages are not set to scale automatically, then it would be sensible to specify the size of the Book Page, so the full Book Page can be displayed within the lightbox area, without the need for scrollbars

For reference, an example of a Link Tile that displays a Book Page in a lightbox (using the settings shown in the screenshot in Step 8 above) is shown below.

★ Using a slider control for the **Lightbox Sizing** option makes absolutely no sense, as these are discrete selections; a drop-down list would have been more logical. Hopefully this will change in a future release.

● Whether Book Pages zoom to fit the container or not is defined in the **Tools | Settings | Playback Settings | book reader | Visual Properties | Zoom for Desktop Playback** property in *Producer*. For all configurations except Mobile, you should consider setting this to **Zoom to fit**.

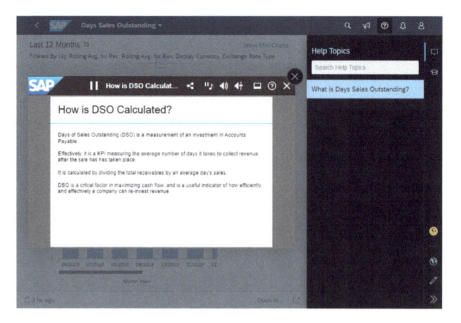

11. If you want the linked object to be opened automatically when the user first accesses the application page (with which the Link Tile is associated) then complete the following fields:

+ Prior to Version 2.4.4 the **Show as Announcement** field was named the **Splash** field.

   i. Select the **Show as Announcement** option. Otherwise, make sure this option is not selected, and the user has to click on the Link Tile itself to display the object.

     Note that if you have multiple Link Tiles with this option selected on the same application screen, then only the first one of these (in **Sequence** order) will be displayed as an announcement.

+ The **Occurrences** option was introduced in Version 2.3.34.

   ii. In the **Occurrences** field, choose whether the announcement should be displayed *every* time the user accesses the screen (**Show always**), or only the first time they access the screen after logging on (**Show only once**).

12. Click **Apply**.

13. Click on the **Save Changes** button to save your Tile.

14. Click on the **Edit Mode** button to exit from the editor.

Save Changes

Your Link Tile has now been created. Don't forget to publish it, as explained in *Publishing Help Content* on page 96.

Changing a Help Topic

To change a Help Topic—whether this is one that you previously created (as explained above), or is standard content that you want to 'extend' and update—carry out the steps shown below.

1. Make sure the *Carousel* is displayed, showing the *Help Topics* page that contains the Help Tile you want to change.

2. Click on the **Edit** button, to switch into Edit Mode.

3. Click on the Tile that you want to change and then select **Edit** from the pop-up menu.

4. The *Edit Content* dialog box is displayed. Make your changes as explained in *Creating a Help Tile* on page 65 or *Creating a Link Tile* on page 76, as appropriate.

5. Click **Apply** in the *Edit Content* dialog box to confirm your changes.

   Tip:
   If you change a 'standard' Help Tile (to 'extend' it), a colored bar is shown on the leftmost edge of the Tile in the *Carousel* to indicate this, as shown in the example below (on the **My Tasks** tile). This is only visible in Edit Mode (users will not see it).

   ➕ The colored bar only appears in Edit Mode; users will not see it (prior to Version 2.4.5 it was also visible to users).

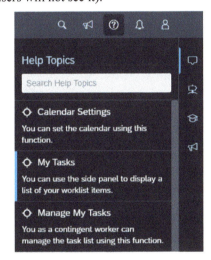

6. Click on the **Save Changes** button to save your changes.

7. Click on the **Edit Mode** button to exit from the *Editor*.

Save Changes

Your Tile has now been changed. Note that you still need to publish your changes as explained in *Publishing Help Content* on page 96.

Deleting a Help Topic

To delete help content (either a Help Tile or a Link Tile) from the *Help Topics* page, carry out the following steps.

1. Make sure the *Carousel* is displayed, showing the *Help Topics* page that contains the Help Tile you want to delete.

2. Click on the **Edit** button, to switch into Edit Mode.

3.   Click on the Help Tile that you want to delete, and select **Remove Tile** from the pop-up menu.

4.   Save and publish your changes as usual.

Note that the *Help Topics* page will continue to be displayed even if you delete the last Help Tile on it. To remove the *Help Topics* page itself, click on the **Options** button and select **Remove Help** from the pop-up menu. You can also use this method to delete all content on the Help Topics page at the same time.

Changing the order of Help Tiles

When you create Help Tiles they are added to the end of the Tile list in the *Carousel*. You can reorder Tiles by entering a new sequence number in the **Change Order** field on the *Tile* tabbed page, during editing. You can also change the order of Tiles directly from the *Carousel*. In Edit Mode, hover the cursor over the Tile you want to move, and a small 'sequence' tab is shown on the lower-right of the Tile, as shown in the example below.

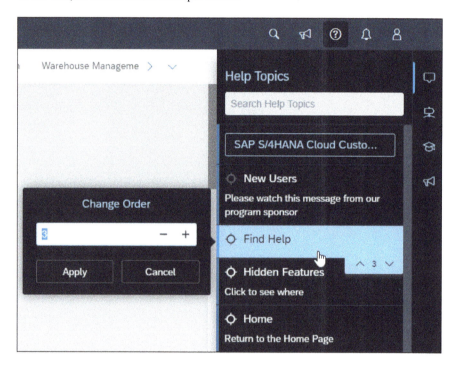

The current sequence of the highlighted Tile is shown in the sequence tab. In this example, the "Find Help" Tile is the third tile on the Carousel.

Click on the **Up** or **Down** button to move the highlighted Tile up or down in the sequence (and therefore in the *Carousel*). Be careful when moving a Tile multiple positions. Don't just blindly keep clicking in the same place, because the Tile the cursor is hovered over will change as the Tiles are reordered. Alternatively, you can click on the sequence number itself to display the *Change Order* dialog box (as shown above) and enter the position of this Tile in the input field. This is usually quicker if you want to move the tile several positions.

You can also move Steps in a Guided Tour in the same way.

Providing Guided Tours

A Guided Tour provides the user with step-by-step instructions on how to complete a task in the application. It is possible to have multiple Guided Tours for a single screen or function—for example, to cover multiple scenarios.

Creating a Guided Tour

To create a new Guided Tour, carry out the steps shown below.

1. In the application, navigate to the page on which you want to start the Guided Tour.

2. Click on the **Edit** button, to switch into Edit Mode. (When you are in Edit Mode the button appears 'selected' [highlighted].)

Edit

3. Click on the **Add** button and select **Add Tour** from the drop-down menu. The *New Tour Name* dialog box is displayed.

Add

4. Enter the name you want to give to your new Guided Tour in the **Name** ("Enter Tour Name") field, and then click **Apply**. This name will appear in the *Carousel* on the *Guided Tours* page, so make it concise, and as meaningful as possible.

   A new Tile is added to the *Carousel*. This is your Guided Tour. It will initially be empty. You now need to record the steps for it.

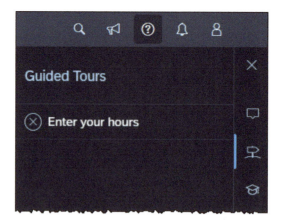

5. Click the **Add Tour Step** button (this looks exactly the same as the **Add** button you clicked in Step 3, but now it has been contextualized for use within a Guided Tour). The *Edit Content* dialog box is displayed.

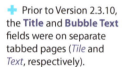 Prior to Version 2.3.10, the **Title** and **Bubble Text** fields were on separate tabbed pages (*Tile* and *Text*, respectively).

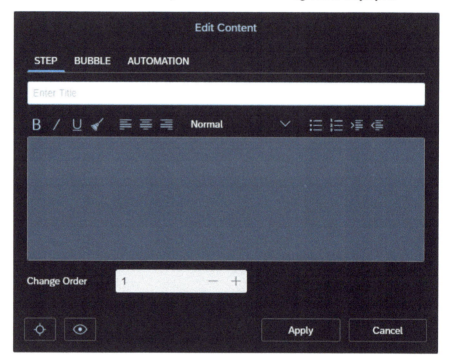

6. On the *Step* tabbed page, enter a short title for the step in the **Bubble Title** ("Enter Title") field. This can appear as a header (in bold) in the Guided Tour Step Bubble, but only if you choose to display it (which, oddly, you can't do from this tabbed page—see Step 21 below).

7. In the **Bubble Text** (text area) field, enter the text that you want to appear in the Bubble for this Step. Try to keep this information short, and to the point. If you need to provide more than a few sentences, consider providing secondary information in a linked Book Page.

The toolbar above the text area provides some standard functions for formatting your text. More functionality is available—for example, to include objects, tables, links and so on—just not from here. See *Chapter 4, Using the Web Editor* for details of this functionality.

8. By default, this new step will be inserted after any currently-defined steps. If you want the step to be inserted at another position in the Guided Tour, then enter or select the step at which it is to appear in the **Change Order** field. (Don't worry if you don't know the exact step number—you can always change this later.)

9. Most of the time, you will want your Guided Tour Step Bubble to point to a specific element on the screen. The next few steps assume you want to do this. If you do *not* want to assign the Step to a screen element (in which case the Step Bubble will be displayed in the middle of the screen), you can jump directly to Step 16 below).

10. Click on the **Assign Hotspot** button in the lower-left corner of the *Edit Content* dialog box.

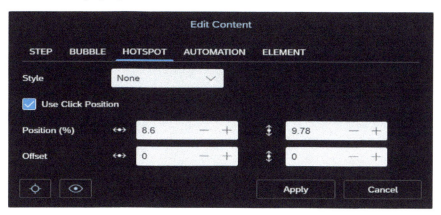

Assign Hotspot

11. The *Edit Content* dialog box is hidden (so you can see the full application page), and the cursor changes to a cross-hairs. Locate and click on the required screen element. When doing this, be sure to follow the guidelines explained in the section on assigning a Hotspot to a Help Tile, on page 68.

12. When you click on the screen element, the *Edit Content* dialog box is re-displayed, as shown below:

This will now have two additional tabs: *Hotspot* and *Element*. Select the *Hotspot* tab. As with Hotspots for Help Tiles, the contents of this tab will depend upon the value selected in the **Hotspot Style** field. However, here there are only three **Style** options:

♦ **None**: No highlighting is used.

♦ **Rectangle**: See *Hotspot Style: Rectangle* on page 72.

♦ **Underline**: See *Hotspot Style: Underline* on page 73.

■ For Guided Tours, it is recommended that you use a **Style** of **None**, so that users aren't distracted by extraneous graphics. Having the Bubble pointing to the element should be sufficient.

● For Guided Tours, the rectangles and the underline do not have the clickable 'corner tab' the way they do for Help Tiles.

13. Select the appropriate style to use for the Hotspot for this Step from the **Style** field's drop-down. The following steps assume you use the default **Hotspot Style** of **None**. Refer to the pages noted above for instructions on using **Rectangle** or **Underline**.

14. By default, the Bubble pointer (or Bubble edge, if no pointer is displayed) will be located exactly where you clicked on the screen. The **Use Click Position** checkbox is automatically selected to reflect this, and the exact position within the element at which you clicked is shown in the **Position (%)** fields. You can move this point (and therefore the Bubble pointer position) by updating these fields. Refer to the note *Using Position fields* on page 72 for instructions on how to use these fields.

15. If you want to 'shift' the Bubble pointer (either relative to the center of the screen element, or relative to the clicked position if the **Use Click Position** option is selected), you can do so by changing the **Offset** fields. This is useful if the Bubble would otherwise obscure the area of the element the user needs to interact with. Refer to the note *Using Offset fields* on page 72 for instructions on how to use these fields.

16. Click on the **Bubble** tab, to show the Bubble-specific controls.

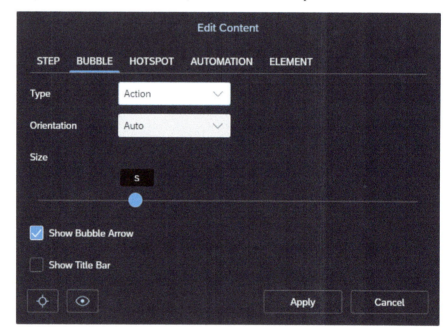

In earlier versions, the *Bubble* page only contained the **Size** field.

The **Show Title Bar** option was added in Version 2.3.32.

17. You can choose to have an icon displayed in the Step Bubble, by selecting the appropriate icon from the **Type** field drop-down. The graphics below shows the available options, and what the Bubble looks like for each of them:

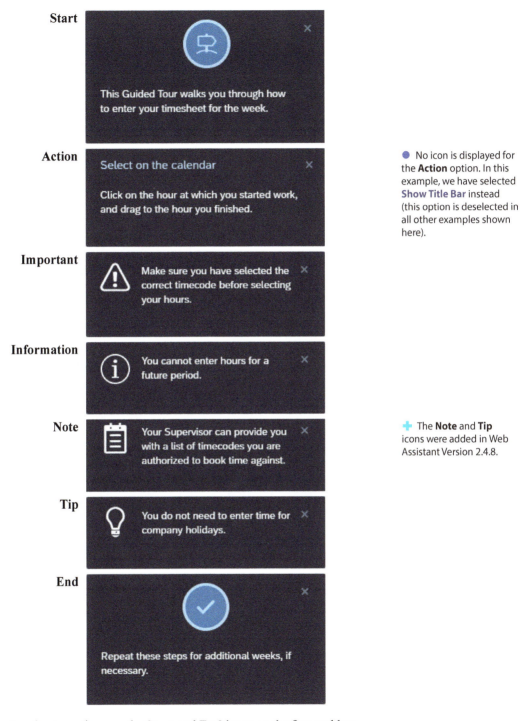

Start

This Guided Tour walks you through how to enter your timesheet for the week.

Action

Select on the calendar

Click on the hour at which you started work, and drag to the hour you finished.

● No icon is displayed for the **Action** option. In this example, we have selected **Show Title Bar** instead (this option is deselected in all other examples shown here).

Important

Make sure you have selected the correct timecode before selecting your hours.

Information

You cannot enter hours for a future period.

Note

Your Supervisor can provide you with a list of timecodes you are authorized to book time against.

✚ The **Note** and **Tip** icons were added in Web Assistant Version 2.4.8.

Tip

You do not need to enter time for company holidays.

End

Repeat these steps for additional weeks, if necessary.

As a best practice, use the **Start** and **End** icons on the first and last Bubbles in the Guided Tour—and use these Bubbles to explain the task and indicate the end of the tour, respectively; do not simply add these icons to the first and last (action) Steps. Use other icons sparingly—they will lose their impact if every Step has an icon.

18. The **Orientation** field defines the position of the Bubble relative to the element (that you clicked on in Step 11). This defaults to **Auto**, which means that SAP Enable Now will determine the optimal position for the Bubble. If you want the Bubble to have a specific orientation, then select this from the drop-down list. The options available are **North**, **East**, **South**, and **West**.

19. If necessary, you can adjust the proportions of the Bubble displayed for this Guided Tour Step by dragging the **Size** slider to **XS**, **S**, **M**, **L**, or **XL**. Bubbles are always automatically sized to accommodate the full **Tile Title** and **Tile Text** entered on the *Step* tabbed page. This setting defines the relative *width* of the Bubble, so a value of **XL** will result a wide but relatively short (height) Bubble, and a value of **XS** will result in a relatively narrow, but taller Bubble. These are 'relative' values (not absolute pixels) so you may need to play around to find the size that works best for this particular Bubble.

● You cannot change the length of the Bubble pointer.

20. If you want the Bubble to have a short pointer that points to the element you clicked on, then make sure that the **Show Bubble Arrow** checkbox is selected. Otherwise, deselect this checkbox.

Note: If you choose not to show the pointer, then the Bubble will still be positioned near (and possibly overlapping) the element; if this is not what you want, you can use the **Position (%)** and **Offset** fields to move the Bubble to another location (see Steps 14 and 15, above), or just select **Center on Screen** from the *Step Actions* pop-up to position the Bubble in the middle of the screen.

21. If you want the **Step Title** (entered on the *Step* tab in Step 6) to be displayed in the Bubble, then select the **Show Title Bar** option. Otherwise, make sure this checkbox is not selected. (See the example of an 'Action' step above to see how this looks during playback.)

22. Click on the **Automation** tab. An example of the *Automation* tabbed page is shown below:

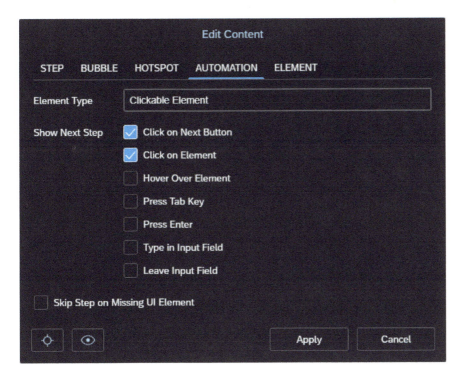

Edit Content

STEP   BUBBLE   HOTSPOT   **AUTOMATION**   ELEMENT

Element Type   Clickable Element

Show Next Step   ☑ Click on Next Button

                   ☑ Click on Element

                   ☐ Hover Over Element

                   ☐ Press Tab Key

                   ☐ Press Enter

                   ☐ Type in Input Field

                   ☐ Leave Input Field

☐ Skip Step on Missing UI Element

Apply   Cancel

23. The settings on the *Automation* page are used to specify under what circumstances the Guided Tour should automatically advance to the next Step. Under **Show Next Step**, select the checkbox for each action that should advance the tour to the next Step. For example, if the current Step is telling the user to click on a button, you might want to automatically advance when the user actually clicks on this button, so would select **Click on Element**. You can select as many or as few options as you think are needed, although obviously not all options will apply to every element type.

➕ The **Show Next Step** feature was added in Version 2.3.26.

24. If this Guided Tour Step should only be shown if the screen element (to which the Hotspot was assigned) is present on the current application page (any part of the page, not just the visible portion) then select the **Skip Step on Missing UI Element** checkbox. This is useful for conditional elements that may not always be present.

➕ The **Skip Step on Missing UI Element** option was added in Version 2.3.27.

25. Click **Apply**. Your step is added to the Guided Tour in the *Carousel*, as shown in the example below.

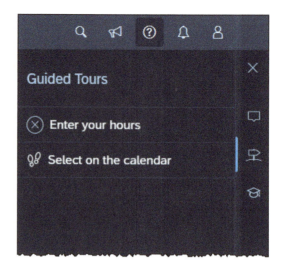

26. Repeat the previous steps to add more Steps to your Guided Tour, until you have described all steps in the task.

27. Once you have finished creating your Guided Tour, click on the **Save Changes** button to save your Tour.

Save Changes

28. Click on the **Leave Tour Edit Mode** button to the left of the Guided Tour name in the *Carousel* to exit from this Guided Tour.

⚠ It is strongly recommended that you test your Guided Tour thoroughly before you publish it.

Leave Tour Edit Mode

29. If you are ready to publish your tour now, click on the **Options** button at the bottom of the *Help Stripe*, and select **Publish Tour** from the pop-up menu. Alternatively, skip this step and you can come back to it later (refer to *Publishing Help Content* on page 96).

30. Click on the **Edit Mode** button to exit from the editor.

Changing a Guided Tour

To change an existing Guided Tour, or to 'extend' a standard Guided Tour, carry out the following steps:

1. Open your application to the page on which the Guided Tour starts.

2. Click on the **Edit** button, to switch into Edit Mode. (When you are in Edit Mode the button appears 'selected' [highlighted].)

Edit

3. On the *Help Stripe*, click on the **Guided Tours** button to list the available Guided Tours.

4. In the *Carousel*, click on the Guided Tour you want to change. The selected Guided Tour will open and all of the Steps in the Tour will be listed in the *Carousel*.

5. If you want to make changes at the Guided Tour level, click on the **Options** button. The following additional options are available on the pop-up menu:

Options

   ♦ **Rename Tour**: Use this option to rename the Guided Tour.

   ♦ **Hide Tour**: Stop the Guided Tour from being listed in the *Carousel* for users. This should normally only be done as a temporary measure (for example, until a specific process goes into effect). You will need to 'unhide' the Tour before users can see it.

   ♦ **Publish Tour**: Make the Guided Tour available to users.

   ♦ **Remove Tour** (for custom content): Delete the entire Guided Tour (see *Deleting a Guided Tour* on page 92).

   ♦ **Remove Tour Extension** (for edited standard content): Remove your edits and return the Guided Tour to its original (SAP-provided) version (see *Deleting a Guided Tour* on page 92).

● If you delete the only Guided Tour, then when you save your changes the entire *Guided Tour* page will be removed and the **Guided Tour** button will no longer be displayed on the *Help Stripe*.

6. To change an individual Step within the Tour, click on the Step in the *Carousel*, and the following options are available from the pop-up menu:

   ♦ **Assign Hotspot** Assign a Hotspot to the Step, if you did not assign one earlier, or want to change the screen element to which the Hotspot is assigned.

   ♦ **Center on Screen** (only available if a Hotspot has already been defined for the Step): Remove the Hotspot assignment.

   ♦ **Edit**: Open the *Edit Content* dialog box, from where you can make any required changes, as explained under *Creating a Guided Tour* on page 83.

   ♦ **Remove Tile**: Remove the selected Step from the Guided Tour.

   ♦ **Discard Changes**: Cancel any changes you have made to the Step since you last saved.

● If you delete the only Step in a Guided Tour, then when you save your changes the entire Guided Tour is removed.

7. Once you have finished changing the Guided Tour, click on the **Save Changes** button.

Save Changes

8. Click on the **Leave Tour Edit Mode** button to the left of the Guided Tour name in the *Carousel* to exit from this Guided Tour.

Leave Tour
Edit Mode

9. If you are ready to publish your changes now, click on the **Options** button at the bottom of the *Help Stripe*, and select **Publish Tour** from the pop-up bubble. Alternatively, skip this step and you can come back to it later (see *Publishing Help Content* on page 96).

Deleting a Guided Tour

If you no longer need a Guided Tour, you can delete it by carrying out the following steps:

1. Click on the **Edit** button, to switch into Edit Mode. (When you are in Edit Mode the button appears 'selected' [highlighted].)

Edit

2. On the *Help Stripe*, click on the **Guided Tours** button to list the available Guided Tours.

3. In the *Carousel*, click on the Guided Tour you want to change. The selected Guided Tour will open and all of the Steps will be listed in the *Carousel*.

4. Click on the **Options** button on the *Carousel*, and select either **Remove Tour** (for a custom Guided Tour) **or Remove Tour Extension** (for changes to a standard Guided Tour) from the pop-up menu.

Options

5. A confirmation message of **Do you want to remove this tour?** or **Do you want to remove all your modifications and revert to the original tour?** (as appropriate) is displayed. Click **Yes**.

6. The Guided Tour is removed (or reverted) and a confirmation message of **Removed successfully** is displayed. Click on the **Save Changes** button.

Save Changes

7. If you are ready to publish your changes now, click on the **Options** button, and select **Publish Help** from the pop-up bubble. Alternatively, skip this step and you can come back to it later (see *Publishing Help Content* on page 96).

Providing a What's New page

As explained in *Chapter 1, An Introduction to Web Assistant*, the *What's New* page can be used to provide users with temporary information about new features in the application, notifications of the availability of new help, and so on.

On the *What's New* page, you can create Help Tiles, Link Tiles, and even Guided Tours in exactly the same way as you can for the *Help Topics* page. However, it is important to understand that this content should be considered as temporary. You can neither select existing help content to be 'featured' on the *Whats New* page, nor *directly* 'move' content from the *What's New* page to the 'regular content' pages (although it is *technically* possible, as explained in *Converting What's New content to 'regular' help content* on page 148). You should therefore always build What's New content with the expectation that it is deleted after a period of time (for example, when it is no longer considered 'new').

Enabling What's New

For SuccessFactors, you specifically have to enable the What's New option so that the *What's New* page is visible in the *Carousel*. For details of how to do this, refer to *Setting up SuccessFactors* on page 52.

For other systems (most notably, S/4HANA systems), the *What's New* page is automatically available as soon a this page is added to the *Help Stripe* (see *Adding the What's New page*, below).

Adding the What's New page

The *What's New* page is not automatically available in the *Carousel* (even in Edit Mode, and even if it is 'enabled'). You first need to add it to the *Carousel* for an application page on which you want it to appear, before you can add content to it.

To make the *What's New* page available for an application page, carry out the steps shown below:

1. In your application, navigate to the page for which you want to provide the *What's New* page.

2. Make sure you are in Edit Mode.

3. Click on the **Add** button, and select **Add What's New** from the pop-up menu. The *What's New* page is added to the *Carousel* (and the **What's New** icon will be visible in the *Help Stripe*).

Add

You can now add content to the *What's New* page as explained in *Adding help content to the What's New page*, below. Note that once the *What's New* page has been published, it will be visible to users—even if there are no tiles on it. You should therefore make sure you add content to the *What's New* page before you save and publish the page.

Adding help content to the What's New page

All of the content types discussed so far in this chapter (Guided Tours, Help Tiles, and Link Tiles) can be added to the *What's New* page. You create them in exactly the same way as described in this chapter, and they all work the same way for users. The only differences are that the content is only visible if the user clicks on the **What's New** icon on the *Help Stripe*, and What's New content uses a different color scheme (by default, although you could configure it to use the same color scheme as 'regular' content—see *Chapter 8, Customizing Web Assistant*).

● You can also 'force' the display of the What's New page by specifying the `whatsNewDirect` parameter.

To add content to the *What's New* page, carry out the steps shown below.

1. In the application, navigate to the page for which the What's New content should be displayed.

2. Make sure the *Carousel* is displayed, and that you are in Edit Mode.

3. Make sure the *What's New* page is displayed (if it is not available, add it as explained above).

4. Click on the **Add** button, and select the appropriate option depending on the type of help you want to add.

Add

5. How you proceed depends upon the type of help that you are adding to the *What's New* page. Refer to the relevant section listed below, as appropriate:

   ♦ *Creating a Help Tile* on page 65.

   ♦ *Creating a Link Tile* on page 76.

   ♦ *Creating a Guided Tour* on page 83.

6. Once you have finished creating your What's New content, click on the **Save Changes** button.

7. Exit from Edit Mode, and then publish your changes as explained in *Publishing Help Content* on page 96.

Save Changes

Removing What's New content

★ To retain your What's New content as 'regular' help content, refer to *Converting What's New content to 'regular' help content* on page 148.

When you decide that you no longer need content on the *What's New* page, you can remove it in exactly the same way as for 'regular' content—by selecting it in the *Carousel* and then selecting **Options | Remove Tile** or **Remove Tour** / **Remove Tour Extension** as appropriate. However, unlike the *Help Topics* page and the *Guided Tours* page, the *What's New* page will continue to exist even if it has no content. To remove the *What's New* page, you have to display the (empty) *What's New* page in the *Carousel*, then click on the **Options** button and select **Remove Help** from the pop-up menu.

Controlling the display of the What's New page

There are a number of parameters that apply to the What's New feature. This section explains what these are and how to use them.

Displaying a What's New announcement

Although the **What's New** icon only appears on the *Carousel* when What's New content is available, users may not necessarily notice it and could miss important information. To help draw their attention to this information, you can display a notification message informing them that What's New information is available. The message is displayed at the top of the screen, and looks like this:

● This text message is fixed, and cannot be changed or configured.

If the user clicks on this message then the *Carousel* is displayed and opened to the *What's New* page.

To enable this functionality, use the following parameter setting:

```
infoBarTimeoutWhatsNew=<s>
```

where `<s>` is the number of seconds for which the message will be displayed, before being automatically dismissed.

■ Because the What's New announcement will only be displayed if What's New content is available for the screen, if you use this feature you might want to leave it always set; this will be easier than changing the parameters in the application every time you add or remove What's New content—especially if you do not have access to change the application parameters yourself.

This message is displayed the first time (during a user's application session) that a user accesses the application page for which What's New content is available. If there is no *What's New* page for the current page, the message will not be displayed. The message will not be re-displayed on subsequent uses of the same page within the same session.

There is an alternative parameter of:

```
showWhatsNew=true
```

that you could specify instead of the **infoBarTimeoutWhatsNew** parameter. This has the same effect, but does not allow you to specify a time limit (although it seems to default to ten seconds).

★ The **showWhatsNew** parameter has likely been deprecated, and may be discontinued in a future release, as there is nothing it can do that can't be achieved through the use of the more flexible **infoBarTimeout** WhatsNew parameter

Displaying the What's New page automatically

If you think there's still a chance your users might miss the What's New announcement (see above), you can force the *Carousel* to be displayed and opened on the *What's New* page, when the user accesses the associated application page. To do this, specify the following parameters:

```
whatsNewDirect=true
whatsNewExpiration=<YYYY-MM-DD>
```

where `<YYYY-MM-DD>` is the date after which the *What's New* page will not automatically be displayed. This is useful if you want to force display of the What's New page for (for example) the first week after implementation of the system or new functionality.

Providing content on the Learning page

Learning content is not created *within* Web Assistant—and is often created for use outside of Web Assistant. For Web Assistant all you are doing is making this content *available* from the *Carousel*. See *The Learning page* on page 13 for more information on how this content is displayed in the *Carousel*.

To make training content available on the *Learning* page of the *Carousel*, you need to designate a Workarea as being the **Learning App** for Web Assistant. You do this by specifying the `learningAppBackendUrl` and `learningAppWorkspace` parameters in the Web Assistant configuration—see *Chapter 2, Enabling Web Assistant*. Once this has been done, the *Learning* page will be available in the *Carousel*, and will automatically list all training material in the designated Workarea that is applicable to the current application page.

Clicking on the **Learning Center** button on the *Learning* page will display all learning content available in the Workarea in a separate browser tab. That is, unless you have identified another source as the Learning App, by specifying the `learningCenterUrl` parameter. This will not affect the *Learning* page, only the *Learning Center*.

Because learning content is not maintained within Web Assistant—and may not even be used from within Web Assistant—it is not covered by this book. Instead, you are directed to the companion book *SAP Enable Now Development* which provides complete instructions on how to create learning content (including Simulations, Books, Book Pages, Quizzes, and more).

Publishing Help Content

Any changes you make to the Web Assistant help are effectively made in a 'development' version of the help system. They do not become visible to the users until you *publish* them (although they will be visible to other Authors). This is useful as it allows you to test and review help content before you make it publicly available.

Before publishing, it is important to know exactly what you will be publishing. You publish one 'Project' at a time. All of the Help Tiles (including Link Tiles) for a single application page are saved to a single Project, which means that you cannot publish only a single Help Tile on a page—you either publish all of them or none of them. You can tell if the Project for the currently-displayed help content is unpublished ('draft') because the **Status** indicator will be yellow, as shown here. If the content has been published, the **Status** indicator will be green (see the example at the end of this section).

Status (Draft)

By contrast, each Guided Tour is stored in a separate Project. This means that you can only publish one Guided Tour at a time—but you must publish the entire Tour. Because of this, the **Status** icon is not shown for the *Guided Tours* page. Instead, the status of each Tour is indicated separately in the Guided Tour list, as shown in the example below:

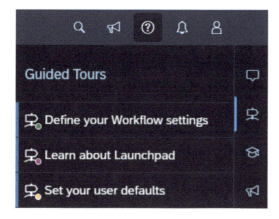

The color-coded dots on the Guided Tour icons have the following meanings:

- **Green**: The Guided Tour has been published.

- **Magenta**: The Guided Tour is new and has not been published.

- **Yellow**: The Guided Tour is an existing Tour that has been changed, and the changes have not been published.

How you publish help content is largely the same, regardless of whether it is a Guided Tour or a Help Topic. To publish help content, carry out the steps shown below.

1. Make sure you are in Edit Mode (click on the **Edit Mode** button if you are not).

2. To publish Help Topics (Help Tiles and Link Tiles), make sure you are on the *Help Topics* page. To publish a Guided Tour, make sure the steps of the specific Guided Tour you want to publish are displayed in the *Carousel* (not just that you can see the Guided Tour on the *Guided Tours* page).

3. Click on the **Options** button on the *Carousel*. The following pop-up menu is displayed:

Options

● This screenshot shows the *Options* menu for Help Topics. The options listed on the menu will be different for a Guided Tour—but both versions contain a 'publish' option.

4. For Guided Tours, select **Publish Tour** from the pop-up menu. For Help Topics, the option you select is **Publish Help**. A confirmation message similar to the example below is displayed (note that it will refer to "tour" and not "help" for Guided Tours).

5. Click **Yes**. The help content is published, a confirmation message is briefly displayed at the top of the screen, and the **Status** indicator changes to green, indicating that this content has now been published.

Status
(Published)

6. Click on the **Edit** button to exit from Edit Mode.

Summary

You can provide several types of information in the Web Assistant *Carousel*:

- Help Topics, which includes Help Tiles and Link Tiles
- Guided Tours, which provide step-by-step instructions on how to execute a specific task in the application
- What's New content, which can be Help Topics and/or Guided Tours that are only available for a limited period
- Learning content, which can be taken from a connected Workarea, or other information source.

You can create help content directly from within the *Carousel Editor*. You can also edit standard SAP-delivered content, if necessary.

You have to publish new or changed help content before it is visible to users.

4

Using the Web Editor

From the *Carousel Editor*, the *Bubble* tabbed page provides basic formatting for **Bubble Text**, such as font formatting, alignment, and so on. If you need to perform some more advanced editing then you can do this via the *Web Editor*. The *Web Editor* is a 100% browser-based application accessible from the *Carousel* or from *Manager*. It provides advanced editing functionality you can use to enhance your help content.

In this chapter, you will learn:

- How to access the *Web Editor* from the *Carousel*

- How to edit help content object properties

- How to insert tables, placeholders, hyperlinks, images, and videos into a Help Bubble

This chapter only covers editing *help content* using the *Web Editor*. It does not cover the editing of *learning content* (such as Simulations, Books, and Book Pages)—partly because this is a much bigger topic, but mainly because it is much easier to create and edit learning content using *Producer*. This is already covered in great detail in the book *SAP Enable Now Development*.

✦ There is rumor that the *Web Editor* may eventually be the primary editor, even from within *Producer*, where it would replace both the *Project Editor* and the *Book Page Editor*.

Accessing the Web Editor

To access the *Web Editor*, carry out the steps shown below.

1. In the application, navigate to the page for which you want to edit the help content.

2. Open the *Carousel*, and display the help content you want to edit—either the *Help Topics* page, the *What's New* page, or a specific Guided Tour (so you can see the Steps within the Tour, not just the list of Tours).

3. Make sure you are in Edit Mode, and then click on the **Options** button on the *Help Stripe*, to display the *Options* pop-up menu.

Options

■ Don't be fooled by the name; this does not take you into the *Manager* (or anywhere near it). However, the *Web Editor* is also used for editing content within the *Manager*, hence the terminology used here.

4. Select **Edit in Manager Web-Editor** from the *Options* menu. The *Web Editor* is opened in a separate browser tab. The content of the *Web Editor* is explained in *The Web Editor screen*, below.

The Web Editor screen

The *Web Editor* allows you to edit a single (complete) Help Project. All Help Tiles for a single application page are contained in a single Project, as are all What's New Tiles. Each Guided Tour is contained in a separate Project.

An example of a typical *Web Editor* screen is shown below:

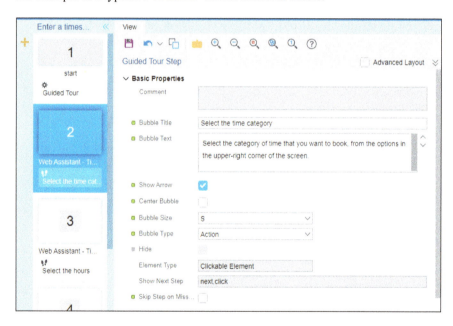

The *Web Editor* screen consists of three components: the *Step View* on the left, the *Macro Editor* on the right, and a *Toolbar* across the top. Let's look at each of these components in more detail.

The Step View

The *Step View* shows the overall 'structure' of the Project, and provides access to all of its constituent parts. Typically, there is one or more numbered Steps, each of which contains one or more 'macros'.

For Guided Tours, the Project will contain one 'content' Step per Tour Step, and each Step contains only one macro, which contains the Tour Step definition. For Help Tiles (including Link Tiles) there will be only one 'content' Step, which is linked to the application page to which the help applies. This content step contains one macro for each Help Tile.

In addition to the content Steps, each Help Project contains an additional first Step named **Start**, which contains only a SETTINGS macro. Although there are properties for both the **Start** Step and the SETTINGS macro that you can display by clicking on them, none of these properties make a difference to Web Assistant content, so we will not cover them here.

Clicking on a Step or a Macro in the *Step View* will show the properties for that Step or macro in the *Macro Editor* pane. We'll look at the *Macro Editor* pane in detail, in *The Macro Editor* on page 102.

The Web Editor Toolbar

The *Web Editor Toolbar* provides access to a few key functions. These are explained in the table below.

Button	Name	Purpose
💾	**Save**	Save your changes. You should always do this before you close the *Web Editor* browser tab.
↩ ⌄	**Multifunction**	The drop-down arrow for this button provides access to several common editing functions. The button itself defaults to the last function used. The full list of functions is shown below:

- ↩ Undo
- ↪ Redo
- ✂ Cut
- 📋 Copy
- 📋 Paste
- 🗑 Delete

Button	Name	Purpose
	Duplicate	Copy the currently-selected Step or macro and insert it immediately below the original.
	Display Bubble	Irrelevant; a hold-over from a previous implementation of the *Web Editor*.
	Zoom (multiple)	Irrelevant; a hold-over from a previous implementation of the *Web Editor*.
	Help	Display the in-application help for the *Manager*. This is pretty much useless here, as you're not even in the *Manager* component.

✦ The *Web Editor* previously replicated the full *Producer Project Editor*, and had a WYSIWYG panel showing the screenshot for a Step. This has been removed (along with the option to change the View Layout, but some buttons which had a purpose in the old *Web Editor* are still shown, even though they have no use now. You can ignore them.

The Macro Editor

The *Macro Editor* pane displays the properties of the object (Step or macro) that is currently selected in the *Step View*. The type of object selected is shown in the upper-left corner of the pane header (in the example below, this is "Tile").

The properties you see listed in the *Macro Editor* generally correspond to the settings in the various tabs of the *Edit Content* dialog box you see when editing directly from the *Carousel*. There are typically many properties for each element type (reflecting the large degree of control SAP Enable Now affords over elements). To simplify the display, and avoid overwhelming new or occasional Authors, the *Macro Editor* initially shows only the most important or commonly-used properties. To display *all* properties, select the **Advanced Layout** checkbox in the upper-right corner of the pane.

■ This book assumes that you are always using the Advanced Layout. If you do not see a property mentioned in the book on your screen, check that you have the **Advanced Layout** checkbox selected.

We'll look at all of the available properties later in this chapter, but there are a few things worth knowing about property definitions and how to change them before you delve into using trying to use them. Let's look at these by way of an example.

The screenshot on the next page shows the *Macro Editor* for a Help Tile (using the **Advanced Layout**).

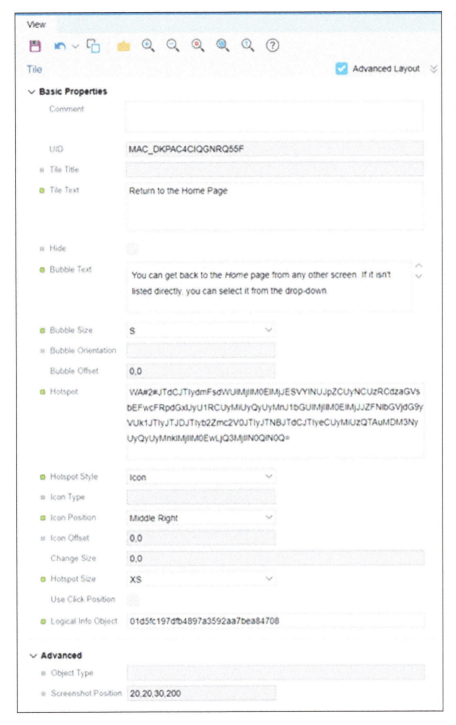

View

Tile   ☑ Advanced Layout ⌄

∨ **Basic Properties**

Comment

UID   MAC_DKPAC4CIQGNRQ55F

▪ Tile Title

▪ Tile Text   Return to the Home Page

▪ Hide

▪ Bubble Text   You can get back to the *Home* page from any other screen. If it isn't
                     listed directly, you can select it from the drop-down.

▪ Bubble Size   S   ⌄

▪ Bubble Orientation

▪ Bubble Offset   0,0

▪ Hotspot   WA#2#JTdCJTlydmFsdWUlMjlIM0ElMjJESVYlNUJpZCUyNCUzRCdzaGVs
                     bEFwcFRpdGxlJyU1RCUyMiUyQyUyMnJ1bGUlMjlIM0ElMjJZFNlbGVjdGlvbjdG9y
                     VUk1JTlyJTJDJTlyb2Zmc2V0JTlyJTNBJTdCJTlyeCUyMiUzQTAuMDM3Ny
                     UyQyUyMnklMjIlM0EwLjQ3MjllIN0QlN0Q=

▪ Hotspot Style   Icon   ⌄

▪ Icon Type

▪ Icon Position   Middle Right   ⌄

▪ Icon Offset   0,0

Change Size   0,0

▪ Hotspot Size   XS   ⌄

Use Click Position

▪ Logical Info Object 01d5fc197dfb4897a3592aa7bea84708

∨ **Advanced**

▪ Object Type

▪ Screenshot Position 20,20,30,200

You can change the width of the *Macro Editor* pane by hovering the cursor over the leftmost border until the cursor changes to a two-headed arrow, then clicking and dragging the divider to the required position.

To the left of most properties is an **Active** indicator. If a property is available for editing, the **Active** indicator appears as a green square (as is the case for most of the properties in the example above). If a property is not available for editing, then this indicator appears as a gray square (as is the case for the **Hide** property in the example above), and the property's value is taken from the default settings.

> ### Where are the default property settings defined?
>
> The default values for macro properties are defined in *Producer* via menu option **Tools | Settings | Authoring Settings | Macro Initialization**. However, the *initial* settings are defined in **Tools | Settings | Playback Settings | Macro Fallback Settings**. When you record a Simulation, the values specified in the **Authoring Settings** are used. If you deselect the **Active** indicator for a property, then its value is set to the **Macro Fallback Settings** value.

Just because a property shows as inactive does not mean that you cannot change it. You just need to click on the **Active** indicator to activate the property first, and then it will be available for editing. Think of the **Active** indicator as being like a 'safety cover' on a physical switch—it is there to make sure you don't *accidentally* change the property value from the default value. It also has the advantage that if you decide you don't want to keep your changes to a property you can just deselect its **Active** indicator and the property will be reset to the default value.

How you change the value of a property will depend on the property that you are changing, but most fall into one of the categories shown below.

For properties that provide a **text box** (regardless of whether this a single line, or multiple lines), type the required value into the text box. For some properties (typically those that can include a lot of text), you may be passed into the full *Text Editor* to edit the text.

● The *Text Editor* is described starting on page 109.

For properties with a **drop-down field** (indicated by a downward-pointing arrow inside the rightmost edge of the field), click in the field and then select the required value from the drop-down list.

For properties with a **checkbox** for a value, simply click on the checkbox to select or deselect it, as required. Selected means 'True', 'Yes', or 'Do this', depending on the item.

Available Properties and their use

Everything that can be done to influence the look and feel of Guided Tours and Help Tiles in the Web Assistant is done through the *Macro Editor*. However, not all properties are available for each type of help content. The table below lists all possible properties, explains their use, and indicates the type of content to which they are applicable.

Property	Use	Guided Tour	Help Tile	Link Tile	
Basic properties					
Comment	Not available for editing; unused.	○	○	○	
UID	Unique identifier of this macro. Cannot be changed.	○	○	○	
Tile Title	This is used in the Tile and in the Bubble. You can change it here, if necessary.		●	●	
Tile Text	This is the main text used in the Tile itself, and appears immediately below the **Tile Title**. You can change it here, if necessary. This is simple text; you cannot apply any formatting to it.		●	●	■ You can prevent the **Tile Text** from being displayed in Help Tiles by specifying the parameter `showShortDescription =false`.
Link to	This specifies the URL of the object to be displayed when the user clicks on the Tile. If you are linking to SAP Enable Now content (in the same Workarea) then you can click on the **Link** button to the right of the field to navigate to and select the relevant content object (which could be a Simulation, Book, Book Page, or Media Objects).			●	
Show Bubble Title	Select this option to have the **Bubble Title** shown in the Step Bubble. This property is named **Show Title Bar** in the *Carousel Editor*.	●			✚ The **Show Bubble Title** option was added in Version 2.3.32.
Bubble Title	This is used in the Step Tile and (optionally) in the Bubble. You can change it here, if necessary.	●			
Bubble Text	This property contains the full text of the Bubble that is displayed for Help Tiles and Guided Tour steps. The *Web Editor* provides many more features than are available in the *Carousel* editor, such as using styles, and inserting tables, images, placeholders, and so on. Refer to *Using the Text Editor* on page 109 for full details.	●	●		■ You can use the up/down arrows on the right of the text box to increase the size of the text box.

Property	Use	Guided Tour	Help Tile	Link Tile
Show Arrow	Determines whether the Bubble includes a pointer, pointing to the Hotspot (or to the Step Tile on the *Carousel*, if there is no Hotspot).	●		
Center Bubble	Select this option to center the Bubble on the screen.	●		
Bubble Size	The size of the Bubble (**XS**, **S**, **M**, **L**, or **XL**).	○	●	
Bubble Orientation	Defines the position of the Bubble relative to the screen element.	●	●	
Bubble Type	Determines the type of icon (if any) to be shown in the Bubble. Options are **Start**, **End**, **Important**, **Information**, **Note**, **Tip**, and **Action**. Refer to page 86 for examples of each option,	●		
Bubble Offset	You can use the X,Y values in this field to shift the location of the Bubble reference point (the tip of the arrow or the center point of the Bubble) relative to the Hotspot (or Icon).		●	
Hide	Can be used to suppress the visibility of a Tile or Step.	●	●	●
Object Image	This property *seems* to work, in that you can select an object from your Workarea (the File Upload part doesn't work) but the image can't be used anywhere, so don't bother. (You can insert it into the **Bubble Text** via a Placeholder, but it is not actually displayed in the Bubble).	○		
Hotspot	Technical information identifying the tethered object. Do not change.	○	○	
Hotspot Style	Specifies the visual type of Hotspot displayed for the help tile. For Help Tiles this can be one of **Circle**, **Rectangle**, **Underline**, or **Icon**. For Guided Tour Steps it can be **Rectangle** or **Underline**.	●	●	
Icon Type	Applies to a **Hotspot Style** of **Icon** only. This field identifies the specific icon that will be displayed. Refer to *Hotspot: Icon* on page 74 for examples of each option.		●	
Icon Position	Applies to a **Hotspot Style** of **Icon** only. This field identifies the position of the icon relative to the screen element.		●	

➕ **Bubble Offset** was introduced in Version 2.3.10.

● How to use a Placeholder is explained in *Inserting a Placeholder* on page 115.

➕ **Hotspot Style** and **Hotspot Type** were introduced in Version 2.3.10.

Property	Use	Guided Tour	Help Tile	Link Tile
Change Size	Applies to a Hotspot Style of **Rectangle** or **Underline** only. Specifies the number of pixels by which the width and height of the Hotspot should be increased (a positive value) or decreased (a negative value).	•		
Use Click Position	If selected, the Bubble pointer will be positioned at the exact location within the element on which you clicked during Hotspot assignment.	•		
Icon Offset	Applies to a Hotspot Style of **Icon** only. This field specifies the (X,Y) offset of the icon relative to the Icon Position.	•	•	
Hotspot Size	Applies to a Hotspot Style of **Circle** only. The size (**XS**, **S**, **M**, **L**, or **XL**) of the circle overlaid on the associated screen object.	•		
Show in Lightbox	Selected if the linked content is to be displayed in a lightbox over the application screen. Otherwise the content will be displayed in a new browser tab.			•
Lightbox Size	If Show in Lightbox is selected then this property specifies the portion of the screen in which the lightbox will be displayed. See Step 10 of *Creating a Link Tile* on page 76 for an explanation of the available options.			•
Width, Height	If the Lightbox Size is set to **User-Defined** or **User-Defined (Overlay)** then specify the height and width of the lightbox, in pixels.			•
Show as Splash Screen	Select this option if you want the linked object to be opened automatically when the user first accesses the application screen (with which the Link Tile is associated). Note that this is different from automatically-displayed What's New content.			•
Element Type	The type of screen element to which the Hotspot is assigned. This is used in conjunction with the Show Next Step parameter for Guided Tour Step automatic advancement.	○		

✚ **Use Click Position** was previously named **Use Click Offset**. It serves the same purpose.

Property	Use	Guided Tour	Help Tile	Link Tile
Logical Info Object	A 'hashed' value that identifies the screen object associated with the Hotspot. Generated from the **Recognition Rule** and **Element Selector** on the *Element* tabbed page of the *Carousel Editor*. Do not change this value!	○	○	○
Show Next Step	Specifies the actions that will cause playback of the Guided Tour to automatically progress to the next Step. Oddly, cannot be changed here, and must be changed via the *Carousel* editor (on the *Automation* tabbed page).	●		
Skip Step on Missing UI Element	If this checkbox is selected, then the Guided Tour Step will not be displayed if the target element (identified in the **Hotspot** property) is not present on the current application page.	●		
Advanced				
Object Type	Irrelevant for Web Assistant; ignore.	○	○	
Screenshot Position	Irrelevant for Web Assistant; ignore.	○	○	
Action	Irrelevant for Web Assistant; ignore.	○		

● Available and used. ○ Available but not functional.

Editing content in the Web Editor

Make any necessary changes to the help as described in *Available Properties and their use* above. Note that you are generally limited to editing existing content (created in the application).

You can insert a new Step via the **Add** button in the upper left of the *Step View*, but you cannot insert new macros into this. The only way to add a new macro from here would be to **Duplicate** an existing macro in another Step, and then drag that onto your new Step. And even then, you would not be able to assign a Hotspot, so it's really better to create Tiles and Guided Tour Steps using the *Carousel Editor*, and then just use the *Web Editor* for some advanced tweaks to the **Bubble Text**.

Using the Text Editor

When you click in the **Bubble Text** property field, you are passed into the *Text Editor*. (If you are familiar with *Producer*, then the *Web Editor Text Editor* is functionally identical to the *Project Editor Text Editor*.)

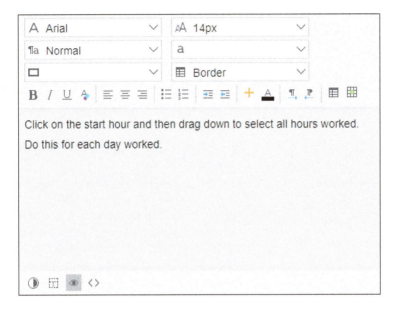

You can change the **Bubble Text** simply by editing the text in the large text area of the dialog box. Click anywhere outside the dialog box to close it again. Whatever you enter in here will be included in the relevant Bubble. This is very intuitive, so isn't described here. Instead, let's look at the other editing functions.

● Text is spell-checked dynamically, within this text area (and within the value fields for any text properties). Any errors are identified by a red wavy underline (the same as for most Windows applications). There is no separate spell-checking function within SAP Enable Now.

The Text Editor Toolbar

There are a number of buttons immediately above the text area. The table below explains what each of these are used for. Most of these are standard and will be familiar to anyone who has used any modern application that allows text formatting (such as Word, PowerPoint, Google Docs, and so on), but for the sake of completeness we'll list them all here.

Button	Name	Purpose
B	**Bold**	Set the currently-selected text to bold.
I	**Italics**	Set the currently-selected text to italics.
U̲	**Underline**	Underline the currently-selected text.

Button	Name	Purpose
	Remove Formatting	Remove any direct formatting applied to the selected text (see the additional notes on this under *Using predefined styles* on page 111).
	Align Left	Left-align the current paragraph.
	Align Center	Center the current paragraph.
	Align Right	Right-align the current paragraph.
	Bullets	Format the currently-selected paragraph(s) as a bulleted list.
	Numbering	Format the currently-selected paragraph(s) as a numbered list.
	Indent	Indent the currently-selected paragraph(s). Note that if the paragraph is a list, the paragraph will be formatted as a next-level list (and using nested number/bullet formats if styles have been defined to support this).
	Outdent	Remove one level of indentation from the currently-selected paragraph. The same comments about lists given in **Indent** also apply here.
	Insert Object	Insert an object into the Bubble. Refer to *Inserting Objects* on page 111 for more information.
	Font Color	Change the color of the selected text. Note that the *Text Editor* may not show the text in the selected color, but changes are saved and can be seen when you return to the *Carousel*.
	Left to Right	This is the default option, for languages that are read from left-to-right (most Western languages).
	Right to Left	Select this option if the text is in a language that is read from right-to-left (such as Arabic and Hebrew).
	Table Operations	If you have inserted a table into the text (via the **Insert Object** button) then this button is available and can be used to perform some basic operations on the table as a whole.
	Cell Operations	If you have inserted a table into the text (via the **Insert Object** button) then this button is available and can be used to perform some basic operations on the currently-selected cell.

Using predefined styles

At the very top of the *Text Editor* dialog box are six fields that you can use to apply predefined styles to elements in the Bubble. The six fields (with their on-screen arrangement replicated below) are:

A	**Font family**	AA	**Font size**
¶a	**Paragraph styles**	a	**Character styles**
▢	**Box styles**	▦	**Table styles**

To use any of these, simply select the text (character, paragraph, or table) and choose the required formatting from the field's drop-down.

It is always advisable to use predefined styles (instead of applying direct formatting), because if the style to be used for a specific text element changes later, all of your texts are automatically reformatted as soon as the Master Author changes the Text Style definition.

There are a few more things noting about the **Remove Formatting** button. If you select a portion of the text and then click on this button, it will remove all *direct* formatting that has been applied to the text (that is, any formatting not set via one of the predefined styles; it will not remove any style formatting). This is extremely useful if you have copied and pasted the text in from another source (especially Microsoft Word, which has an annoying habit of applying all kinds of [sometimes hidden] styles to text), and you want to remove all of the source formatting before applying your own styles.

Remove Formatting

Inserting Objects

There are a number of things that you can insert into a bubble, by using the **Insert Object** button. You can insert the following objects:

Insert Object

- Table
- Link
- Placeholder
- Image
- Video

Each of these options has its own peculiarities, so we will look at them separately, below.

★ Text styles are maintained via menu option **Tools | Customization | Edit Text Styles**.

● Of the six style types available here, only paragraph styles are available from within the *Carousel Editor*.

■ If you are pasting content from another application it is usually easier to right-click and select **Paste as plain text** from the shortcut menu.

Inserting a table

You can insert tables into the Bubble Text—either to provide tabular information, or just to better control the layout of the text. To insert a table, carry out the following steps:

1. Click on the **Insert Object** button and select **Insert Table**. The following dialog box is displayed:

2. Specify the number of rows and columns you want your table to have (including headers) in the **Columns** and **Rows** fields. A table of the specified size will be shown in the right-hand side of the dialog box so you can confirm your specifications.

3. In the **Alignment** field, select how the table should be aligned within the Help Bubble. Note that if you enter a width of 100%, this setting is irrelevant.

4. Select the measurement type to be used from the drop-down list on the right of the **Width** field (valid values are **auto**, **%** and **px**), and then specify the desired width of the table in the leftmost side of the field (as a percentage for **%** and as an absolute number of pixels for **px**).

5. If you want your table to include row and/or column headers, then select the appropriate option in the **Header** field. How these are formatted depends upon the table style used, but a typical default is to have the text in the header cells set in bold, and possibly have the cells shaded.

6. Select the predefined style to use for this table in the **Table Style** field. By default, the options are **None**, **Border**, or **Borderless**. Your Master Author can define additional table styles in *Producer*.

7. Click **OK** to insert the table into the text box.

● Even if you want to use a borderless table, it is recommended that you insert a bordered table so that you can see the cell boundaries when the table is initially empty. Enter your content, and then change the table to a borderless table once you are finished.

Once you have inserted a table, you can use the **Table Operations** button to update the basic table properties (**Alignment**, **Width**, and **Table Style**), delete the entire table, or convert the table to text. You

Table Operations

can also click in a cell and then use the **Cell Operations** button to change the individual cell properties (**Column Width**, **Row Height**, **Cell Background** [color], **Horizontal Alignment**, and **Vertical Alignment**) and add, remove or duplicate rows and columns. You can't set colored borders here, but if your Master Author has defined a table style that uses colored borders, you can apply that style to the table via the **Table Operations** button or via the **Table Style** drop-down.

Cell Operations

Inserting a Link

To insert a text hyperlink to additional content, carry out the following steps:

1. Select the text that should be linked in the editor, then click on the **Insert Object** button and select **Insert Link** from the drop-down menu. This will display the *Insert Link* dialog box, as shown below:

Insert Object

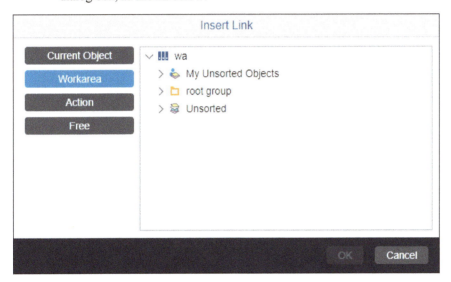

2. In the panel on the left, either click on **Workarea,** to provide a link to a content object that currently exists in your (help) Workarea, or click on **Free** to provide a link to any other location.

● The **Current Object** and **Action** options are irrelevant for Web Assistant help content.

3. The *Insert Link* dialog box is updated depending on your selection:

    ♦   If you selected **Workarea** then the Workarea structure is shown on the rightmost side of the dialog box (as shown in the example above). Navigate to and select the content object you want to link to.

    ♦   If you selected **Free** then a single input field of **Link** is shown on the rightmost side of the dialog box. Enter the target link in this field.

▲ As always, you should only use URLs that you have high confidence will continue to be available.

4. Click **OK** (in the *Insert Link* dialog box). The *Edit Link* dialog box is displayed, as shown below.

5. The **Display Text** field contains the text you selected in Step 1 (to use as the hyperlink). If you did not select any text, then enter the text you want to be used as the link into this field. This text will then be inserted into the Bubble Text at the current cursor position.

6. The **Link Target** field contains either the internal link to the selected Workarea object or the URL, as appropriate. You should not need to change this here, but if necessary (for example, if you return here to edit the link after you have created it), you can click on the folder icon to the right of the field to open the *Insert Link* dialog box again, where you can change the link type and/or target.

7. If necessary, you can enter a ToolTip in the **Tooltip** field. This will be displayed when the user hovers over the link. You might find it helpful to let the user know what type of content will be launched if they click on the link.

8. Select the **Open in New Window** checkbox. If you do not select this checkbox, then the target of the link will be loaded into the current browser window, replacing the application—which you typically wouldn't want to happen.

9. Click on the **Properties** button and specify the format of the new window that will be opened (such as whether scrollbars and so on will be included). This is standard browser functionality so will not be explained in detail here.

10. Click **OK** to close the *Edit Link* dialog box.

If you subsequently need to change the hyperlink, position the cursor in the hyperlink text, and then click on the **Insert Object** button again. This will now have two additional options:

- **Edit Link**: Select this option to display the *Edit Link* dialog box (see above), where you can make any required changes.

- **Remove Link**: Select this option to remove the link (the link text itself will not be deleted, just the hyperlink).

Inserting a Placeholder

A Placeholder allows you to insert another piece of predefined content into the **Bubble Text**. The important thing about this is that if the source of this content changes, the **Bubble Text** is automatically updated. SAP Enable Now provides many types of Placeholders, including allowing you to insert the **Name**, **Description**, or **Short Description** of a related Project, Book, Book Page, or Text Unit. Within the context of a Help Bubble most of these are irrelevant, since there *are* no associated objects. However, there are still a couple of useful applications for Placeholders with Web Assistant help content:

- You can include a standard or common text by using a Placeholder for the **Description** of a Text Unit that contains this text.

- You can include the exact, current name of a linked content object by using a Placeholder for the **Title** of a Book or Book Page.

In the steps below, we'll use the second example.

To insert a Placeholder into your Bubble Text, carry out the steps shown below:

1. If you are inserting a Placeholder that references another object, you need the UID of that object. The easiest place to obtain this from is the **UID** property for the object in *Producer*, as shown below:

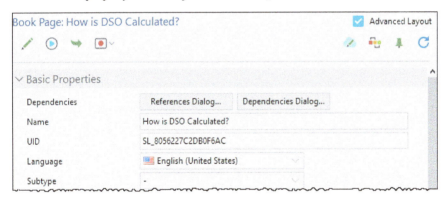

You can select the contents of the **UID** field, and copy it to the clipboard.

2. From within the *Text Editor*, position the cursor where you want the Placeholder to be inserted, then click on the **Insert Object** button and select **Insert Placeholder** from the drop-down menu. The *Select Placeholder* dialog box is displayed. An example of this is shown below.

Insert Object

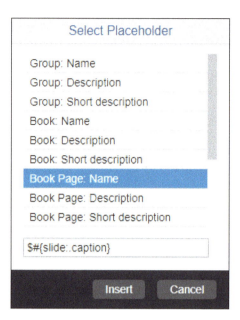

3. Click on the type of Placeholder that you want to insert. This will update the field at the bottom of the dialog box with the Placeholder value (as shown in the example above).

4. The Placeholder value is in relation to the *current* object. You need to update it to specify the actual object you want to reference. Enter an exclamation point (!) followed by the UID you copied in Step 1 in between the object type ("slide" in the example above) and the colon (:), so that the Placeholder value looks like this:

```
$#{slide!SL_8056227C2DB0F6AC:.caption}
```

This can be interpreted as: Insert the **Name** ("caption") of the Book Page ("slide") with a *UID* of SL_8056227C2DB0F6AC into the **Bubble Text**.

5. Click **Insert** to close the *Insert Placeholder* dialog box.

● To do this, first insert the **Name** using a Placeholder, and then select the inserted text and create the hyperlink.

The advantage of doing this is that if the **Name** of the referenced object changes, this will automatically be reflected in your Help Bubble. You could also use a Placeholder as the 'display text' for a link, when linking to an object in your Workarea, for guaranteed consistency.

Inserting an image

You can insert an image into the **Bubble Text**. This can be an image that already exists in your SAP Enable Now Workarea, or an image currently located outside of your Workarea. As a best practice, if the same image will be used multiple times, you should import it into your Workarea and then always insert it from there.

To insert an image into the **Bubble Text** that you are currently editing, carry out the following steps:

1. From within the *Text Editor*, place the cursor where you want the image appear, then click on the **Insert Object** button and select **Insert Image** from the drop-down menu. The *Select Image* dialog box is displayed. An example of this is shown below.

Insert Object

2. In the panel on the left, either click on **Workarea** to insert an image file that already exists in your (help content) Workarea, or click on **Upload File** to upload a new image file (which will then only be usable within this specific Project).

3. The *Select Image* dialog box is updated depending on your selection:

   ♦ If you selected **Workarea** then the Workarea structure is shown on the rightmost side of the dialog box (similar to the example on page 113). Navigate to and select the image you want to insert into the **Bubble Text**.

   ♦ If you selected **Upload File** then the **Choose File** button is displayed (as shown in the example above). Click on this button to display the standard Windows *Open File* dialog box, and then navigate to and select the image file.

4. Click **OK** (in the *Select Image* dialog box). The following dialog box (also titled *Select Image*) is displayed.

● The **Current Object** option is only useful if you want to link to an image that has already been inserted into the **Bubble Text** for another Tile within the same Project.

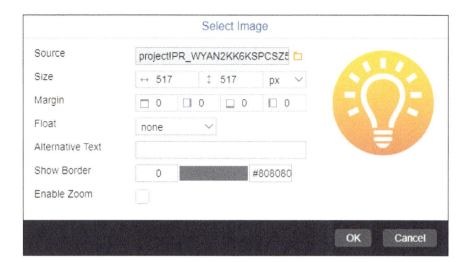

● The **Enable Zoom** option does not seem to work for Web Assistant help content, so is not described here.

5. A copy of the selected image is shown on the right of the dialog box. You can use this to confirm that you have selected the correct file.

6. The **Source** field specifies the identifier of the Workarea object for the image (if you uploaded an image, this will be a sub-object of the Tile macro, within the Help Project). You should not need to change this here, but if necessary (for example, if you return here to edit the image properties after you have inserted it), you can click on the folder icon to the right of the field to open the (first) *Insert Link* dialog box again. You can then select a new image and/or change the image properties (as explained in the next few steps).

7. The **Size** fields default to the original size of the image. If you want to resize the image for display within the **Bubble Text**, then select the sizing unit (**px or %**) from the drop-down field on the right, and enter the new dimensions in the provided **Width** and **Height** fields.

8. If necessary, specify the amount of padding (white space) that should be preserved around the edges of the image in the four **Margin** fields (**Top**, **Right**, **Bottom**, and **Left**, as indicated by the graphic to the left of each field). You may want to specify a few pixels of space to make sure any surrounding text is not too close to the image area.

9. If you want the text in the Bubble to 'wrap' around the image (as opposed to the image appearing on its own line) then select whether the image should be aligned to the **Left** of the Bubble (with text to the right of the image) or to the **Right** (with text to the left), in the **Float** field.

10. Enter a short text description of the image in the **Alternative Text** field. This will be used by ADA-compatible screen-readers, and may be required for compliance purposes.

11. If you want to add a border to the image then select the border width (in pixels) in the first **Show Border** field, and specify the border color either by clicking on the color block in the middle of the property line

and selecting a color from the drop-down swatch, or by entering the hexadecimal RGB value for the color in the input field on the right.

12. Click **OK** to insert the image into the **Bubble Text**.

An example of an image inserted into a Help Bubble is shown below.

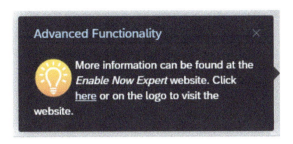

In this example, the image has a *Float* value of **Left**, and a **Right Margin** of **3pt**. This example also shows a link, inserted as explained in *Inserting a Link* on page 113.

If you subsequently need to change the image or its properties, select it in the *Text Editor* and then click on the **Insert Object** button again. The **Insert Image** option will have been replaced by an **Edit Image** option that you can click on to display the (second) *Select Image* dialog box (see above), where you can make any required changes.

Inserting a video

Simulations and Books/Book Pages are all well and good, but sometimes it is more effective to use full-motion video to communicate a message. Handily, SAP Enable Now allows you to play a video directly within a Help Bubble. In this section, we'll look at how to do that.

Unfortunately, you can only insert a video that already exists in your help content Workarea. There is no option to upload a new video, like there is for images. Therefore, you should have already uploaded the video as a Media Object in *Producer*, before continuing.

To insert a video in the **Help Text** for a Bubble, carry out the following steps:

1. From within the *Text Editor*, position the cursor where you want the video to appear, then click on the **Insert Object** button and select **Insert Video** from the drop-down menu. The *Insert Video* dialog box is displayed. An example of this is shown below.

Insert Object

■ If you want to link to a video on YouTube (or other video sharing site), use a Link Tile instead, and have the target video displayed in a lightbox. See *Creating a Link Tile* on page 76 for details of how to do this.

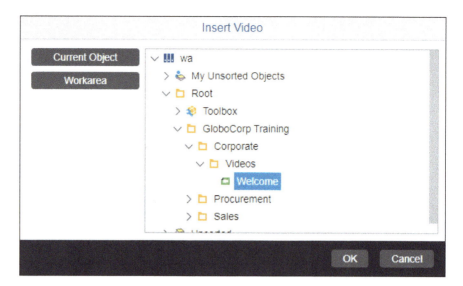

● The **Current Object** option is only useful if you want to link to a video that has already been inserted into the **Bubble Text** for another Tile within the same Project—which you would probably not want to do.

2. Make sure **Workarea** is selected on the left, and then navigate to and select the Media Object for the video you want to include in the Help Bubble.

3. Click **OK** to confirm your selection. A second *Insert Video* dialog box is displayed, as follows:

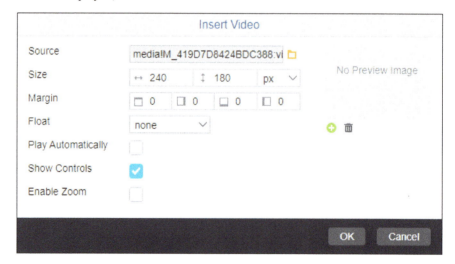

● The **Enable Zoom** option does not seem to work for Web Assistant help content, so is not described here.

4. The **Source** field specifies the identifier of the selected Media Object. You should not need to change this here, but if necessary (for example, if you return to this dialog box to edit the video properties after you have inserted it), you can click on the folder icon to the right of the field to open the (first) *Insert Video* dialog box again, where you can select a new video and/or change the video properties (as explained in the next few steps).

5. On the right is a box containing the text **No Preview Image**. If you want to display a specific image before the video is played then use the **Add** button below this box to navigate to and locate an image file to use. (Inconsistently, here you *can* load an external file.) The selected image will then appear in this box. If you change your mind, you can always use the **Delete** button to remove the preview image. If you do not use a preview image then the first frame of the video will be displayed in the bubble (but not in this box).

   ● Obviously, there is no point in having a preview image if the video is set to play automatically (see **Play Automatically**, below)

6. Specify the size at which the video should be displayed, in the **Size** fields. Select the sizing unit (**px** or **%**) from the drop-down field on the right, and enter the new dimensions in the provided **Width** and **Height** fields.

7. If necessary, specify the amount of padding (white space) that should be preserved around the edges of the video in the four **Margin** fields (**Top**, **Right**, **Bottom**, and **Left**). You may want to specify a few pixels of space to make sure any surrounding text is not too close to the video playback area.

8. If you want any text in the bubble to 'wrap' around the video (as opposed to the video appearing on its own line) then select whether the video should be aligned to the left of the Bubble (with text to the right of the video) or to the right (with text to the left), in the **Float** field.

9. If playback of the video should start as soon as the user displays the Help Bubble then select the **Play Automatically** checkbox. If you do not select this checkbox then you need to select **Show Controls** (in the next step) so the user has some way of starting playback.

10. If you want playback controls to be made available to the user (in a panel at the bottom of the video when the user hovers the cursor over it—see the example at the end of this section) then select the **Show Controls** checkbox. You would typically only deselect this checkbox if the video contains its own controls (where supported by the video format).

11. Click **OK** save your changes and return to the *Text Editor*.

A partial screenshot showing an example of a Help Bubble that contains an embedded video is shown below:

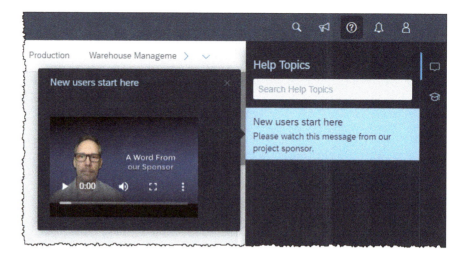

In the above example, the **Show Controls** checkbox has been selected.

If you subsequently need to change the image, select it in the *Text Editor* and then click on the **Insert Object** button again. The **Insert Video** option will have been replaced by an **Edit Video** option that you can click on to display the (second) *Edit Video* dialog box (see above) where you can make any required changes.

Editing the source HTML

Bubble Text is ultimately saved within SAP Enable Now in HTML format, as this provides the most flexibility for converting it into other forms of output. Sometimes it is useful to be able to see—and optionally edit—this underlying HTML. Fortunately, SAP Enable Now provides a feature for doing exactly that.

To switch to HTML mode, simply click on the **Source** button in the *Text Editor*. The dialog box then appears like the example shown below.

★ This example uses the Bubble to which we added a Placeholder in *Inserting a Placeholder* on page 115, and provides a link to the same object, as explained in *Inserting a Link* on page 113.

```
<p>For an example of how DSO is calculated, refer to
<span style="font-style: italic;"><a
href="javascript:ctx.cfg_show('slide!SL_8056227C2DB0F6
AC', null, null);" title="Book Page">$#
{slide!SL_8056227C2DB0F6AC:.caption}</a></span>.</p>
```

Obviously you need to have a working knowledge of HTML to make sense of this view, but if you do, it is helpful for troubleshooting formatting issues, or to force specific formatting.

Click on the **Design** button to return to the regular view.

● All common HTML tags are supported, but not all tag *attributes* are, so be careful with these, because SAP Enable Now will just strip out any code it doesn't like.

Saving your changes

Once you have finished your edits, save your changes and return to the application as follows:

1. Click on the **Save** button on the Toolbar.

2. **Wait** for the following message to be displayed:

    Changes successfully saved.

3. Once you see the confirmation message, you can close the *Web Editor* browser tab and return to the application.

4. Exit from Edit Mode and then refresh the browser screen before navigating away from the current application page or making any further changes to the help content.

Back in the application, you will need to refresh the browser to load your latest changes.

▲ If you immediately edit the help content without refreshing the screen, any changes you made in the *Web Editor* will not be visible. Don't panic—they have still been saved, but you need to refresh the screen to retrieve them.

Summary

If you want to include more than just text in your Help Bubbles (and you should seriously consider doing so, to provide more engaging help), you can use the *Web Editor*. This allows you to edit any of the help objects' properties, provide feature-rich text in the Help Bubble, and insert tables, placeholders, hyperlinks, images, and even videos.

You can do all of these things using the *Project Editor* in *Producer*, but you will probably find it more convenient to use the *Web Editor* as you can access this directly from the *Carousel*, and the specific help content Project you are editing will be opened for you.

5

Working in Manager

In this chapter, we will delve into the *Manager* component of SAP Enable Now. This is by no means a detailed guide to *Manager* (that will require a separate book all to itself), but is instead a quick look at a few selected Web Assistant related activities that you may need to perform in *Manager*.

In this chapter you will learn:

- Where to find your help and learning content in *Manager*
- How to edit help content
- How to 'extend' standard SAP-delivered learning content
- What reports are available for Web Assistant

Accessing Manager from Web Assistant

You can access *Manager* directly by entering its URL into the browser (for cloud implementations of SAP Enable Now) or by starting the desktop component (for on-premise implementations). This is the usual way of accessing it for most purposes. For maintenance of Web Assistant content, you can access *Manager* directly from the *Carousel* (or *Learning Center*). The advantage of this is that you will be positioned directly on the required content object within *Manager*, ready to edit it.

How you access *Manager* from Web Assistant depends upon the type of content you want to access: help content or learning content, so we will look at these two methods separately, in the sub-sections below.

Accessing help content

Within *Manager*, all of the Help Tiles and Link Tiles for an application page are stored in a single Project. Each Guided Tour is stored in its own Project. So to access help content in *Manager*, you first need to be in Edit Mode for the help content Project you want to access—either the applicable *Help Topics* or *What's New* page, or a specific Guided Tour.

With the help content displayed in the *Carousel*, click on the **Options** button, and then select **Show in Manager Workspace** from the pop-up menu. You are passed into *Manager*, and positioned on the Project for the help content.

Options

Accessing learning content

You can access *learning* content (including Books, Book Pages, Simulations, and other context-tagged content objects) either from the *Learning* page in the *Carousel*, or from the *Learning Center*.

■ In the *Learning Center* you may need to click on the **Edit** button in the header to switch (back) into Edit Mode. If you *are* in Edit Mode but the **Feedback** button is shown, use the **Category** buttons to switch to a different category and back again, and that should refresh the display.

In both cases, if you are in Edit Mode you will see a 'folder' icon in the lower-right corner of the content tile, as shown in the two examples below. This is the **Show in Manager Workspace** button. (In Display Mode, the **Feedback** button is displayed here, instead.)

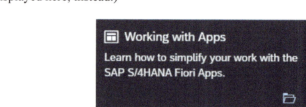

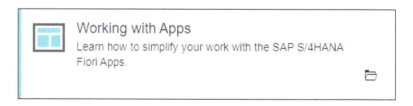

Click on the **Show in Manager Workspace** button. You are passed into *Manager*, and positioned on the Project for the selected learning content object.

The Manager Interface

The *Manager* screen consists of two sections: the *Object Navigation Pane* on the left, and the *Object Editor Pane*—which shows the details of the currently-selected content object—on the right. An example of a typical *Manager* screen is shown below.

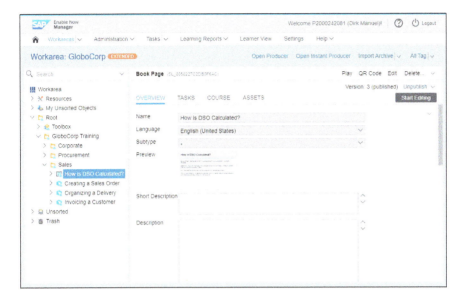

The *Object Navigation Pane* shows the entire contents of the Workarea, organized into a hierarchy. The organization of this content will depend upon the purpose of the Workarea—whether you use it just for help content, just for learning content, or for both. As always, it is simpler to consider help content and learning content separately.

Help content in Manager

Initially, all help content (Projects for Help Tiles or Guided Tours) will be created under **Unsorted**. The Project name will correspond to the application's **Help Key**. This is typically the application page identifier—which is also shown in the *Help Context Information* dialog box (refer to the example on page 62). For help content created by editing the standard SAP-delivered content in an Extended Content Scenario, the Project name will be appended with the text "(Extension)".

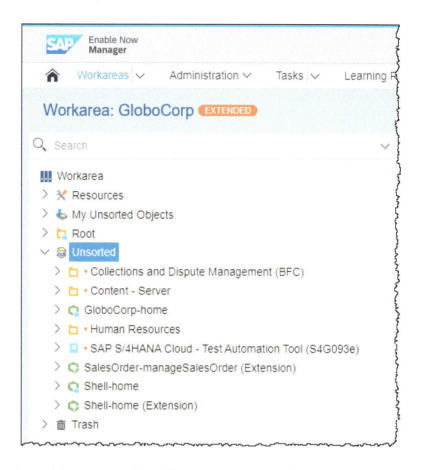

In the partial screenshot of the *Object Navigation Pane* above, you can see that there are *two* Projects for the application page **Shell-home** (this is the S/4HANA *Home* page). This is a fairly unusual situation, but it does illustrate a few important points that are worth discussing in a little detail, before we continue.

The first of these Projects—the one just called **Shell-home**—was created under a Custom Content Scenario (`serviceLayerVersion=WPB`), and is pure 'customer-created' help content. The second one—called **Shell-home (Extension)**—was created under an Extended Content Scenario (`serviceLayerVersion=EXT`) by 'extending' the standard content. Both of these were created for the same application page, but they are two entirely separate Projects. The important thing to understand here is that only one of these two Projects will be displayed to the user via the *Carousel*. Which one this is will depend upon the setting of the `serviceLayerVersion` parameter at the time the help is displayed.

To complete the story, if the **Shell-home (Extension)** Project was deleted (or was never created in the first place), the SAP-standard version—which is also called **Shell-home**—would appear in its place—even if `serviceLayerVersion=EXT` (because no 'extended' version exists). This standard version would also be displayed if

> serviceLayerversion=UACP was used—even if **Shell-home (Extension)** still existed because UACP always uses the standard version.

The less-obvious impact of this is that if you create help content under the Custom Content Scenario (WPB), and then switch to the Extended Content Scenario (EXT), you will not see your previously-created help content—because it was created under a different scenario! The same applies if you create content by extending the SAP-standard content in EXT mode and then change to WPB mode, as a way of only using only *some* of the standard SAP content. Because of this, it is extremely important to decide which scenario you want to use before creating *any* help content, and then create *all* of your help content within that scenario.

Organizing your help content

As noted above, all help content is initially created in the **Unsorted** Group—and with no organization to this (other than alphabetical order). This is not normally a concern, since the structure of Help Projects within the Workarea is never visible to users. You *could* move this content under **Root**, or organize it into sub-Groups, but from a *functionality* point of view there is little advantage to doing this. If you have a separate Workarea dedicated to your help content there is no need to move your help content out of **Unsorted**. Most of the time you will maintain this content from the *Carousel*, and even if you do need to edit the content object in *Manager*, you can use the **Show in Manager Workspace** option to easily locate the object, regardless of whether it is stored in **Unsorted** or anywhere else. However, if your help content shares a Workarea with your learning content, you may want to keep **Unsorted** empty, and your **Root** appropriately organized.

One other circumstance under which it may be useful to re-organize your help content is when you are localizing it. In this case, you might want to store the help content for each language in its own Group, to make localization and maintenance easier (you can localize content at the Group level). Refer to *Chapter 7, Localizing Your Content* for more information on localizing help content.

Learning content in Manager

All learning content (Books, Book Pages, Simulations, and so on) should be located under **Root**, typically organized into a logical structure through the use of Groups. This is desirable as users will see (at least some portion of) this structure if they access the *Trainer* (either directly or via the **Learning Center** button if the *Trainer* has been specified on the `learningCenterUrl` parameter). However, for **Extended** Workareas, the standard SAP-provided learning content can typically be found under **Unsorted**, in a Group named **Content - Server**. You can move this (or just the sub-sections for the content that applies to your specific product and version) to somewhere under **Root** if necessary. Whether you do so or not largely depends upon whether you want users to see the standard content in

● If you only want to use a subset of the SAP-provided content, you will need to use EXT mode, and extend and then hide all the help content you *don't* want to use. This will require constant vigilance as SAP frequently adds new content (sometimes without notification), which will then be displayed by default unless you hide it (or extend it).

the *Trainer*. Only content in the **Root** group (or other Group used as the *Trainer* 'entry point') will appear in the *Trainer*; content in **Unsorted** will not. However, any context-applicable content will always appear on the *Learning* page of the *Carousel* and in the *Learning Center*, regardless of where in the Workarea it is located.

This last point raises an interesting potential inconsistency, in that users could see a learning content object on the *Learning* page, but then be unable to find this same object via the **Learning App** button. This could happen if you use the *Trainer* as your Learning App, but not all of your user-accessible content is located hierarchically below your *Trainer* entry point. You should consider this possibility when deciding how to organize your learning content—and in particular for standard content in an **Extended** Workarea.

Changing standard learning content in Manager

If you are working in an Extended Content Scenario then all of the SAP-provided learning content (in the underlying **Connected** Workarea, from which your own Workarea is **Extended**) will potentially be visible to your users. You have the ability to change this content to better reflect your company's needs. Changing standard learning content is effectively done in the same way as changing your own content (and, honestly, is easier to do in *Producer*), but there is an additional step required if you do this in *Manager*. This is to 'fetch' this content from the (**Connected**) SAP standard Workarea into your own (**Extended**) Workarea. You need to do this before you can change the content. Let's look at this by way of an example.

First, let's suppose you have accessed the *Learning Center*, and see the following content listed:

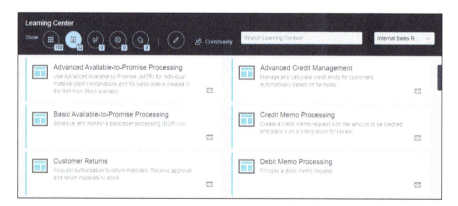

Assume you identify the *Customer Returns* Book Page as learning content you want to use, but want to change it, to tailor it to your company's specific needs. Before you can change this content object, you need to copy it into your extended Workarea. Do this as follows:

1. In the *Learning Center*, click on the **Edit mode** button to switch into Edit Mode. The **Send feedback to author** (envelope) button in the lower-right of the content tile will change to the **Show in Manager Workspace** button (a 'folder' symbol), as shown below:

Edit mode

2. Click on the **Show in Manager Workspace** button. You are passed into *Manager*, and positioned on the Project for the selected help content.

● *Manager* will be opened in a new browser tab—even if you already have *Manager* open in another tab.

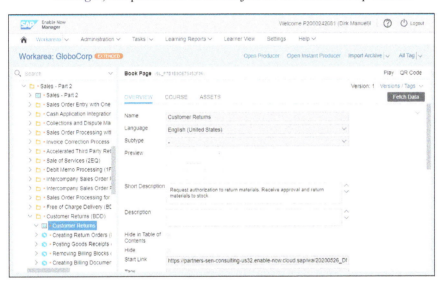

There are a few things worth noting here:

♦ To the right of the Workarea name at the top of the screen is an orange lozenge that says "**Extended**". This indicates that this Workarea is based on another Workarea (the standard SAP one).

● For instructions on how to set your Workarea as being based on a standard (SAP-provided) Workarea, refer to *Organizing your Workareas* on page 25.

♦ Most of the content objects listed in the *Object Navigation Pane* have an orange dot to the left of the object name, as shown here for the object we want to change:

This indicates that the object exists in the underlying standard Workarea. The dot is the same color as the **Extended** indicator, to provide you with an additional visual clue—although really it should be purple to indicate that the content is currently located in the **Connected** Workarea.

- There is a gray button labeled **Fetch Data** on the upper-right of the *Object Editor* pane for the selected object. The availability of this button (you will not see it for your own content) indicates that this object needs to be 'extended' (copied) into your own Workarea before you can change it.

3. Make sure the content object is selected in the *Object Navigation Pane*, and then click on the **Fetch Data** button. The content object is copied over into your Workarea. The object no longer has an orange dot next to its name in the hierarchy and the icon now contains the familiar 'cloud' indicator, as shown below.

> 🖥️ Customer Returns

You can now edit the content object and make any necessary changes, just as if it were a content object you had created yourself (which, from this point on, it effectively is). Refer to *Editing content in Manager* on page 132 for details of how to edit content.

It is important to note that from this point on, any changes to the standard content object will not be reflected in the copy you now have in your Workarea—which is the version users will see. If you want to incorporate the changes made to the standard version into your custom (extended) version, you have two options:

- Delete your extended version, re-fetch the standard version, and then re-do your changes in this new copy.

- Manually replicate the changes made to the standard version in your extended version.

Reverting a standard content object

■ If you are wondering how you can prevent your users from seeing a standard content object if you can't delete it—you need to hide it, which you can do in the *Carousel Editor* or in *Manager*.

If you decide that you no longer want to have a customized ('extended') version of a standard content object and want to revert to the original, SAP-provided version, you can just delete the custom object in the Workarea. To do this, click on the object to select it, and then select **Delete | Delete** on the upper-right of the screen This will remove your custom version, making the standard version visible again (you cannot delete a standard content object).

▲ To some extent, **Trash** is treated as just another Group in your Workarea, and content in **Trash** can still appear in the Web Assistant. For this reason, you should always remove any deleted help content from **Trash** as a last step. (Alternatively, you can hide the content object before deleting it, if you are not ready to delete it forever, just yet.)

You should also delete your custom object from the server trash. Do this by clicking on the object in the **Trash** Group, and then selecting **Delete | Delete Finally** on the upper-right of the screen.

Editing content in Manager

To edit a content object in *Manager* (regardless of whether this is custom content or standard content that you have 'extended' into your Workarea), carry out the steps shown below.

1. With the content object Project selected in the *Object Navigation Pane* on the left, click on the **Start Editing** button in the upper-right of the *Object Editor* pane (in the place previously occupied by the **Fetch Data** button, for extended content objects). This will check out the object for editing.

2. You can now make any necessary changes to the content object properties (such as its **Name**, **Short Description**, *Web Assistant Context* properties, and so on), by entering the new values in the *Object Editor Pane* on the right. Click the **Save** button to save your changes to the object properties.

3. To change the actual contents of the object, click on the **Edit** link on the toolbar at the top of the *Object Editor Pane*. You are passed into the *Web Editor*. You can now edit the content object as required.

   Instructions on using the *Web Editor* can be found in *Chapter 4, Using the Web Editor*.

   Once you have finished editing the content object, save your changes, then close the *Web Editor* browser tab. You are returned to *Manager*.

4. Click on the **Finish Editing** button on the upper-right of the *Object Editor* pane. The *Finish Editing* dialog box is displayed, as shown below.

● The *Finish Editing* dialog box is very similar to the *Finish Editing* dialog box in *Producer*. The instructions provided here are fairly succinct, assuming that you are already familiar with the *Producer* version. If you are not, refer to *Publishing your changes* on page 167.

5. If you want to change the person to whom the object is assigned, then select the required person in the **Assigned to** field.

6. If you want to change the **Status** property of the object, then select the new status in the **Status** field. (Note that changing the **Status** to **Published** will not necessarily publish the object—see Step 10, below.)

   If a Workflow Process has been assigned to the content object you will not be able to change the **Status** directly, but will need to select the appropriate Workflow action on the *Tasks* tabbed page.

7. Optionally, you can enter a comment—for example, explaining what has changed—in the **Comment** field.

● Watchers are SAP Enable Now users who should be notified about certain events that take place for objects. Watchers are assigned on the *Tasks* page of the *Object Editor Pane*.

● Remember that publishing will be done at the Project level. This means that all Help Tiles for an application page will be published at the same time.

8. If you want the Watchers for this object to be notified via (automatic) email that the object has been edited and checked in, then select the **Send Mail to Watchers** checkbox. Otherwise, make sure this checkbox is not selected.

9. Click **Save**.

10. Back at the *Manager* screen, if the content object should be published now (so that it is made available to users) click the **Publish** link on the toolbar at the top of the *Object Editor Pane*. Users will not see your changes until you publish the object.

> If a Workflow Process has been assigned to the content object this may have been set up to automatically publish the content object when its **Status** reaches a specific value (see Step 6, above). In this case, you do not need to publish the object yourself.

For help content objects you also have the option to publish the content object from the *Carousel*, in Edit Mode.

You can now log out from *Manager* (click the **Logout** link in the upper-right corner of the window) and return to the *Learning* page or the *Learning Center*, depending on where you accessed *Manager* from.

Web Assistant Reports

● It is anticipated that the reporting capabilities of SAP Enable Now will be significantly enhanced in the future. This may include integration with SAP Cloud Analytics.

SAP Enable Now provides several reports that can be used to monitor the use of help content and learning content. Two of these are applicable to Web Assistant: the *Web Assistant Usage Report* and the *All Learner Feedback Report* (which actually applies to *all* content, including Web Assistant). Here, we will look at only these two reports.

The Web Assistant Usage Report

The *Web Assistant Usage Report* provides metrics on the extent to which help content and training content is being referred to by users. For these metrics to be captured (for subsequent inclusion in the report) you need to have the following parameter set:

```
trackingUrlWPB={URL}
```

where **{URL}** is the URL of your help content Workarea.

To generate the *Web Assistant Usage Report*, select menu option **Learning Reports | Web Assistant Usage Reports**. The *Web Assistant Usage Report* is immediately displayed (there is no selection dialog box you need to complete first). An example of this report is shown below.

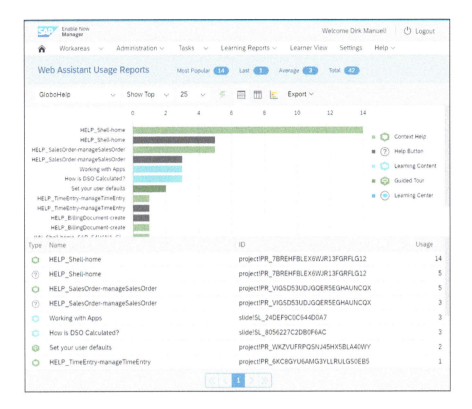

The report initially consists of two main areas: a bar chart in the upper half of the screen, and a table in the lower half of the screen. The information is the same in each of these (just displayed in a different format), and you can choose to display one or both of them via the following buttons:

Icon	Name	Purpose
	View Chart and Table	Display both the chart and the data table on the screen (this is the default view).
	View Table Only	Display only the data table.
	View Chart Only	Display only the chart.

Before looking at how to adjust the report content, let's look at what information is being shown.

Before we start, it is important to understand that the report counts 'hits' at the *content object* level. You may recall that all Help Tiles and Link Tiles for an application page are stored in the same content object (Project). This means that if a user clicks on six different Help Tiles on the same application page, the report will record one 'hit' against the Project for the application page. Similarly, each Guided Tour is stored in a separate Project, so each launch of a Guided Tour will generate a separate entry in the report. This will be counted once, regardless of how many Steps within the Tour the user displayed or interacted with. The same is true of What's New content, even though here Help Tiles and Guided Tours are stored on the same page: displaying the *What's New* page will count as one 'hit' on the What's New Project regardless of how many Help Tiles on the *What's New* page are interacted with, and launching a Guided Tour from the *What's New* page counts as a single hit against the Guided Tour project.

Bearing all this in mind, let's look at the different types of interaction that are captured on the report. These are color-coded, and listed in a key on the rightmost side of the chart (the same icons are used on the leftmost side of the data table). The table below lists all of the possible entry types, and explains what they represent.

Entry Type	Interaction Captured
■ ⑦ Help Button	Clicking on the **Help** button to open the *Carousel*. The **Name** shown in the data table or in the graph data point hover-over pop-up box identifies the application page from which this was done (prefixed with "HELP_").
■ ⬡ Context Help	Either (a) displaying the *Help Topics* page (regardless of whether this was as a result of clicking on the **Help** button to open the *Carousel*, or clicking on the **Help Topics** button on the *Help Stripe*), or (b) displaying the *What's New* page (by clicking on the **What's New** button on the *Help Stripe*). Again, the **Name** indicates the application page from which this was done (in this case, prefixed with "HELP_" for the *Help Topics* page, or "HELP_WN_" for the *What's New* page).
■ ⬠ Guided Tour	Launching a Guided Tour. The **Name** shown is the **Name** of the Guided Tour, but there is no indication as to which application page this was called from.
■ ◉ Learning Center	Clicking on the **Learning Center** button on the *Learning* page of the *Carousel*. The **Name** indicates the application page from which this was done (prefixed with "HELP_").
■ ⬡ Learning Content	Launching a learning content object (such as a Simulation, Book, or Book Page) either from the *Learning* page of the *Carousel* or from the *Learning Center* (there is no indication as to which). Note that this does not include learning content launched through a Link Tile (this is captured under **Context Help**). The **Name** shown is the **Name** of the launched content object.

Entry Type	Interaction Captured
■ 🖼 Learning App	Clicking on the **Learning App** button on the *Learning* page of the *Carousel*. This button is displayed in place of the **Learning Center** button if you have chosen to use an alternative source of learning content as the Learning App (by specifying the `learningCenterUrl` parameter).

★ In the current (2.4.10) release this is not working as described here and the **Learning Center** button is always displayed; hopefully this will be fixed in a future release.

Now you have a better idea of what is (and is not) captured on the report, let's take a brief look at the information and options available in the blue report header.

In the header, you can see some overall metrics about your Web Assistant usage. These are (from left to right):

- **Most Popular**: The number of times the most frequently-used content object was displayed or interacted with.

- **Least**: The number of times the 'least-frequently-used' content object was displayed or interacted with. Note that the report is not able to include content objects that have not been used at all (that is, have a zero 'hit' count), so this may not necessarily be a useful indicator of 'under-utilized' content.

- **Average**: The average number of interactions per content object that has been referred to at least once (again, the report will exclude objects that have not been used at all).

- **Total**: The total number of user interactions with any of the Web Assistant content.

▲ **Total** may be an unreliable metric of specific use, as (for example) closing a Guided Tour will trigger an additional hit on **Total** (only), because the *Carousel* is redisplayed.

Below the summary metrics is a set of controls you can use to influence the records shown on the report. This includes a drop-down to select a specific Workarea (or **All Workareas**), and drop-downs to select the number of unique content objects to list in the report. If you make any changes to these selection fields, click on the **Apply Ranges** button to re-generate the report using your new selection. Finally, there is a drop-down field you can use to export the report (for example, to Microsoft Excel) for further analysis.

Apply Ranges

You can use the information provided on this report to gauge the extent to which your help content (and learning content accessed from Web Assistant) is being used. You may find it useful to identify the specific application pages for which help is being opened most frequently. These are probably the most 'difficult to use' pages of the application, so you should consider providing additional—or clearer—help for these pages.

You may find it useful to monitor the **Total** metric over time, and see if delta usage is increasing or decreasing. However, as there is no ability to generate the report for a specific date range, you will need to export the report data periodically, and perform your own analysis on how the **Total** changes over time.

The All Learner Feedback Report

The *All Learner Feedback Report* consolidates all feedback received from users on learning content. This includes feedback submitted from the *Trainer* as well as feedback submitted from Web Assistant. Unfortunately, there is (currently) no mechanism for users to provide feedback on help content objects.

To generate the *All Learner Feedback Report*, carry out the steps shown below:

1. Select menu option **Learning Reports | All Learner Feedback Report**. The *All Learner Feedback Report* dialog box is displayed.

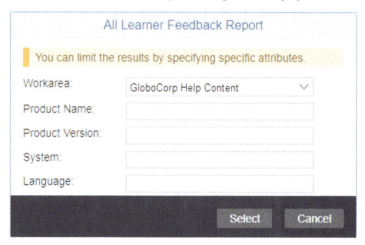

2. In the **Workarea** field, select the Workarea that contains the content for which you want to review the feedback (this should be the Workarea containing your learning content—again, there is no ability for users to provide feedback on help content, so there is no point in specifying the Workarea containing your help content).

   Note that if you have based your own Workarea on one of the SAP-provided standard Workareas you can select the **Connected** Workarea here to report on feedback provided for the standard content. (Feedback submitted by *your* users will be recorded in *your* SAP Enable Now installation, not SAP's.)

3. If necessary, you can specify the application and release for which the feedback has been received in the **Product Name** and **Product Version** fields. If you specify values for these fields, then the report will only include feedback for content objects that have these specific values specified in their *Web Assistant Context* properties at the time the feedback was submitted. Because only such objects will be accessible via the *Learning* page and *Learning Center*, this is a good way to ensure your report only includes content accessible via Web Assistant.

4. If necessary, you can limit the report to showing only feedback received for content objects with a specific language code by entering that

The **System** property has been deprecated and can be ignored.

language code (such as **en-US** for U.S. English) in the **Language** field. This is useful if you have language-specific teams monitoring (and responding to) user feedback.

5. Click **Select**. The report is generated, but is not displayed on the screen because this report is only available for download. The following message is displayed to inform you of this:

   `This report does not visualize data, it is for exporting only. Use the buttons below to export the results in the preferred file format.`

6. Click on the **XLS Export** button or the **CSV Export** button as necessary.

The report is downloaded. Open it in the appropriate application. An example of the *All Learner Feedback Report*, as it appears in Microsoft Excel, is shown below (split into two sections due to size constraints—it's a very wide report).

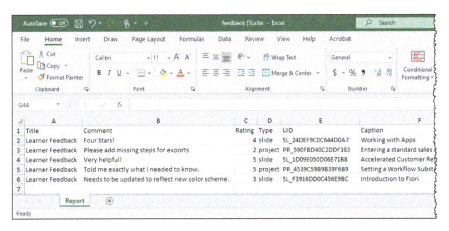

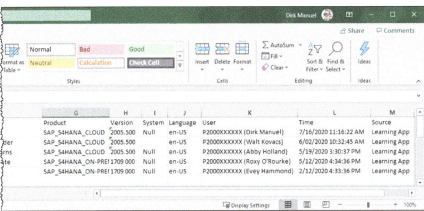

Most of the information provided is self-explanatory, but there are a few fields that are worth paying particular attention to. These are:

- **Comment**: This is the user's free-form comments.

- **Rating**: This is the numerical value of the 'star' rating selected by the user (see *User Feedback* on page 15)

- **Caption**: This is the **Title** of the learning object from which the feedback was submitted.

- **Source**: As noted at the start of this section, the *All Learner Feedback Report* includes *all* feedback submitted by users. This field indicates from where the feedback was submitted. A value of **Learning App** indicates that the feedback was submitted from the *Learning* page of the *Carousel* or from the *Learning Center* so you may want to filter on this value to display only Web Assistant applicable feedback.

You can use the information provided on this report to identify changes you need to make to your learning content. Aside from responding to the comments, you should consider re-working any content that scores a consistently low rating.

Subscribing to the report

You can 'subscribe' to the *All Learner Feedback Report* so that it is automatically generated and sent to you via email, periodically. To do this, carry out the steps shown below.

1. Generate the *All Learner Feedback Report*, as described in the previous section.

2. Once the report has been generated (and you see the message "`This report does not visualize data...`"), click on the **Save...** button on the upper-right of the screen. The *Save Report* dialog box is displayed.

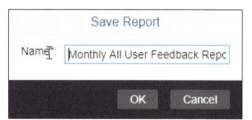

3. Enter a suitable name for your generation of the report in the **Name** field, then click **OK**.

4. You will now see a **Subscribe** button in the upper-right corner of the *All Learner Feedback* screen. Click on this. The *Scheduler* dialog box is displayed.

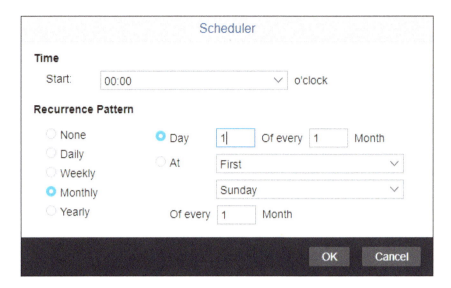

5. Select the time at which the report should be generated, and indicate the frequency with which it should be generated in the fields provided. Note that the fields available on the right will depend upon the frequency selected on the left.

6. Click **OK**.

The report will now automatically be generated as specified, and sent to you as an attachment to an email.

You can change or cancel your scheduled reports by using menu option **Administration | Scheduler**.

Summary

Manager is one of the components of SAP Enable Now. There are no content creation or maintenance related activities that you *need* to perform in *Manager*, and most activities are easier to perform from the *Carousel* or in *Producer*. However, it is often easier to locate a content object in *Manager* than it is to do so in *Producer* (since you can jump directly to the required content object from the *Carousel*).

Most likely, you will only use *Manager* to fetch standard learning content and to make minor changes to content properties. You may also use it for generating and reviewing the two Web Assistant related reports.

6

Working in Producer

In this chapter we will look at Web Assistant related activities that you either can do or need to do in the *Producer* component of SAP Enable Now. This is not an exhaustive look at *Producer* functionality—just a look at the basics as they pertain to Web Assistant content. If you need additional guidance on using *Producer*, the book *SAP Enable Now Development* covers *Producer* in detail.

In this chapter, you will learn:

- How to apply context to learning objects
- How to change the context for help content
- How to 'adopt' standard SAP content
- How to assign content categories and roles to your learning content

The Producer interface

Producer provides access to all of the content available in a single Workarea, including any content in the **Connected** Workarea from which this Workarea is **Extended**. You cannot switch between Workareas from within the cloud version of *Producer* (as you can in *Manager*), so if you use multiple Workareas (for example, one for help content and one for learning content—as explained in

Organizing your Workareas on page 25) you will need to close *Producer* for one Workarea before opening it again for the next Workarea.

An example of a typical *Producer* screen is shown below.

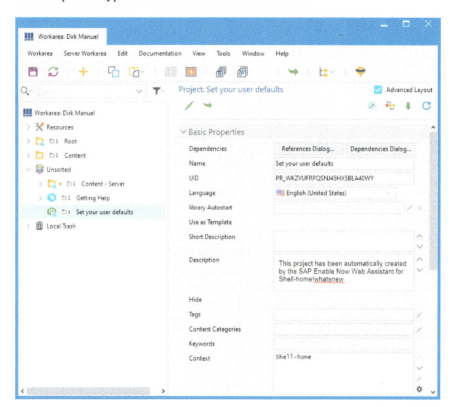

The *Producer* screen consists of three main components. These are identified in the graphic on the right, and explained below.

1. The menu and *Producer Toolbar*, across the top of the screen

● The *Object Navigation Pane* is sometimes referred to in the SAP documentation as the *Project Explorer*, but as not everything in it is a Project, this book uses the term *Object Navigation Pane*.

2. The *Object Navigation Pane*, on the left of the screen

3. The *Object Editor Pane*, on the right of the screen. This lists all of the properties for the currently-selected object. The *Object Editor Pane* has its own *Toolbar*. The buttons on this will depend on the object type.

In this chapter, we will look briefly at the contents of each of these components as we need them. For a complete explanation of all possible contents, please refer to the book *SAP Enable Now Development*.

Locating content in the Workarea

All content in the Workarea will appear somewhere in the *Object Navigation Pane*, where it is organized into a single hierarchy. Each of the highest-level entries (or 'Groups' in Enable Now terminology) in this hierarchy has a specific function. Let's look at each of these.

- The **Resources** Group contains files required by SAP Enable Now to function, including templates, configuration files, scripts, and so on. You should not need to change any of these files (although the Master Author may perform some customization to the objects in this Group).

- For Workareas used for learning content, all of the (custom) training content should be located under the **Root** Group. Note that this Group has a blue 'cloud' symbol in the lower-right corner of its icon. This is important, as it indicates that this Group is synchronized with the central content library on the server.

- The **Content** Group contains objects that only exist in your local storage and not on the server (note that the Group icon does not contain a cloud symbol). You can use this Group for practice, or for creating content that you do not want to save to the server. Content that should be made available to users should not be stored in this Group.

- When you create help content (as described in *Chapter 3, Creating Help Content*) it is saved in the **Unsorted** area, which is effectively just a single Group that contains everything not specifically included under the Workarea **Root**. If your learning content Workarea is **Extended** from one of the SAP-provided standard Workareas, this Group will also contain all the learning content located in the underlying **Connected** Workarea. You can move content from **Unsorted** to somewhere under **Root** if necessary (see *Organizing your Workareas* on page 25 for further discussion on this).

- **Local Trash** contains all content objects that you have deleted in *Producer*. They will remain here until you 'empty' the trash (which you should do, periodically). Even when you delete them from your Local Trash they will remain in the *Manager's* **Trash** on the server until you delete them from there.

Within the *Object Navigation Pane*, each object is identified by its name, and an icon indicating the type of object. A list of the object types (potentially) applicable to the Web Assistant is given in the table below.

● The **Resources** group is only displayed if you select menu option **View | Workarea Details | Show Resources**.

■ You may want to rename this Group to something like "My local content", to better reflect its use.

● The **Local Trash** group is only displayed if you select menu option **View | Workarea Details | Show Local Trash**.

■ You can choose other information to be shown (such as a language indicator) via menu option **View | Workarea Details**.

Icon	Object Type	Description
	Group	Groups are used for organizing content within the Workarea.
Help Content		
	Web Assistant Guided Tour	A Guided Tour Project contains step-by-step instructions on the completion of a task. The object name is the name of the tour as entered by the Author at the time of creation (or subsequent editing).
	Web Assistant Context Help	A Context Help Project contains all of the Help Tiles and Link Tiles (or all of the What's New content) for a single application page. The object name is automatically set to the application page name (Key).
Learning Content		
	Simulation Project	A Simulation Project is a recording of a task being performed in the system. It can typically be played back as a demonstration, an interactive practice exercise, or a concurrent playback designed to guide the user through a task as they complete it in the system.
	Book	A Book is a collection of Book Pages. Typically, Books are used to create courseware presentations.
	Book Page	A Book Page (sometimes referred to as a 'slide') is a single, fixed-size page of information. Book Pages are often grouped into Books, but can be used independently, as stand-alone content objects (even if they are also used within a Book).
	Text Unit	A Text Unit is a (variable length) unit of information that typically contains text, but can also contain graphics, tables, and even videos. Text Units are most effectively used when they are embedded into other content objects (such as Simulations or Book Pages).
	Video Media Object	An external video file (such as .MP4 or .WMP) that has been imported into SAP Enable Now.
	Audio Media Object	An external sound file (such as .MP3) that has been imported into SAP Enable Now.
	Image Media Object	An external image file that has been imported into SAP Enable Now.

Maintaining help content

Although you can edit Web Assistant Projects in *Producer*, it is much easier and more intuitive to do so via the *Carousel Editor* directly in the application (as explained in *Chapter 3, Creating Help Content*). Therefore, this section only covers the things that you can *only* do in **Producer**.

Locating custom help content

As noted above, when you create help content via the Web Assistant *Carousel Editor*, it is stored in the **Unsorted** area of your Workarea. Your local *Producer* typically contains a snapshot of the contents of the server Workarea. This is refreshed when you synchronize. However, this synchronization may not include content in the **Unsorted** area—especially if this is content that has been created by another Author. If you are looking for content that you know exists, but you cannot see it in Producer, you may need to 'check out' this content to make it visible to you. The following steps explain how to do this.

1. Select menu option **Server Workarea | Check Out Objects....** The *Checkout* dialog box is displayed.

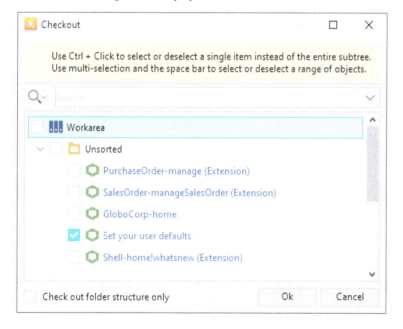

● This is unfortunate terminology, as it will not 'check out' the content objects in the sense of making them available for editing. Instead all the **Check Out Objects** function does is make the objects visible in your *Producer* Workarea.

2. Expand the **Unsorted** folder, and select all of the Web Assistant Help Projects that you want to work with in *Producer*. These will have a green hexagon object icon, as shown in the sample screenshot above.

3. Click **Ok**.

The selected content objects will be copied into your Workarea, and will appear under **Unsorted**. You can now edit them as required.

Converting What's New content to 'regular' help content

When you create What's New help content, it created in such a way that it will only appear on the *What's New* page of the *Carousel*, even though it is created and displayed in exactly the same way as help content on the *Help Topics* page is created.

What's New content is designed to be temporary (and deleted once it is no longer considered 'new'), and is not really designed to be moved from the *What's New* page to the *Help Topics* page once it is no longer considered 'new'. However, there may be circumstances where you want to keep the What's New content you have created and have it appear as regular content under the *Help Topics* page or the *Guided Tours* page (as appropriate). This is not as it is *designed* to be used, but you *can* do it if necessary. How to do this is explained in the steps below.

1. Click on the Web Assistant Project in the *Object Navigation Pane* to select it, and then click on the **Start Editing** button at the top of the *Object Editor Pane*.

Start Editing

2. Locate the **Context** property in the *Object Editor Pane* for the What's New Project, and remove the text **!whatsnew** that immediately follows the application page name.

3. If you are 're-purposing' a What's New Help Tile, then this is all you need to do, and can jump to Step 9. However, for a Guided Tour the context is also recorded at the 'step level' within the Project, so you need to change it there, as well.

4. Open the What's New Guided Tour Project in the *Project Editor* (either double-click on the Project in the *Object Navigation Pane*, or click on the **Edit** button at the top of the *Object Editor Pane*).

Edit

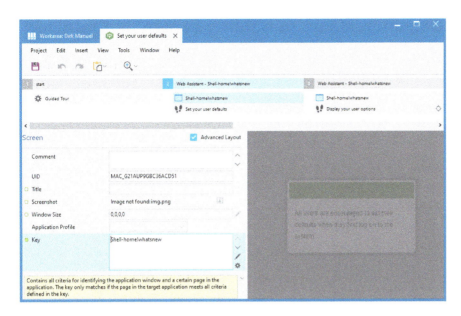

5. Locate the **Screen** macro for the first (or next) Step, and click on it to display its details in the *Property Sheet* (shown on the left in the example above).

6. Edit the **Key** property, and remove the text **!whatsnew**, just as you did at the Project level.

7. Repeat Steps 5 and 6 for all additional screens in the Project.

8. Save and close the Guided Tour.

9. Finish editing the Project, and publish it (see *Publishing your changes* on page 167).

The help content will now appear as 'regular' help content, and will no longer appear on the *What's New* page.

Maintaining training content

Typically, you will create and edit your training content within *Producer*, simply because the *Project Editor* and *Book Page Editor* provided in *Producer* are easier to use than the *Web Editor*. This includes Simulations, Books, and Book Pages.

Creating and editing training content is a much bigger topic than we can cover in this book, so instead we will confine ourselves to the tasks you may need to perform in *Producer* that are specifically related to providing training content within Web Assistant.

★ If all of the **Screen** macros in the Guided Tour are for exactly the same application page, you can use the **Edit | Select Macros By Type** function to select all **Screen** elements, and then change the **Key** property for them all at the same time. Because the **Key** is also used for the **Screen Title**, you can easily check if this is the case by scanning the **Screens** in the *Thumbnail Pane* (shown across the top of the screen in the example above).

Changing standard training content in Producer

As explained in *Where does Web Assistant get its content?* on page 17, you can configure Web Assistant to use your own Workarea as the source of the training content for the *Learning* page of the *Carousel* and the *Learning Center*. If you have defined your Workarea as being **Extended** from one of the SAP-provided standard Workareas, then all of the SAP-provided content in the **Connected** Workarea will also be visible to your users, and will be accessible to you (as the content Author) in *Producer*. Content that is actually located in the **Connected** Workarea is identified by an orange dot in your customer Workarea, as shown in the example below.

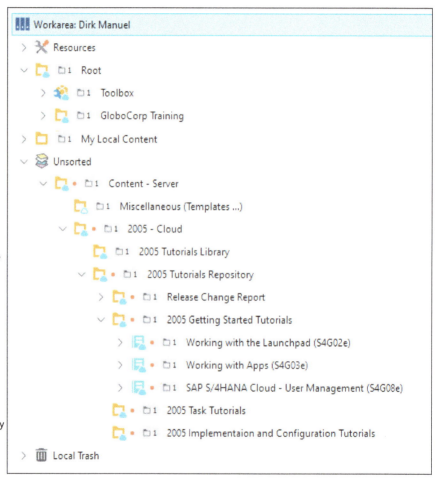

★ If there are content Groups in the connected standard Workarea that you know you will never use (for example, because it is for a version of the system that you do not have), you can right-click on the Group and select **Remove Locally** from the shortcut menu. The content will then be removed, and only the high-level Group left as a placeholder. This is the case for **Miscellaneous (Templates ...)** in this example—note the 'empty cloud' icon used.

In this example, you can see that everything under **Root** (including **Root** itself) exists in the **Extended** (customer) Workarea. By contrast, everything under **Unsorted** exists in the **Connected** standard Workarea. The Resources are also always taken from your own Workarea—even if a copy also exists in the **Connected** Workarea.

To edit a content object that is currently located in the **Connected** Workarea, carry out the steps shown below.

1. Click on the content object (which will have an orange dot to the right of the object icon), to select it.

2. Click on the **Start Editing** button (or double-click on the content object)—just as you would to edit an object in your customer Workarea.

3. The *Get Inherited Objects* dialog box is displayed, as shown below.

Click **Yes**.

A copy of the content object is created in your customer workarea. You will see that the content object now looks exactly like any other content object that has been created in your own Workarea (there is no yellow dot for the object). Compare the screenshot below with the previous example.

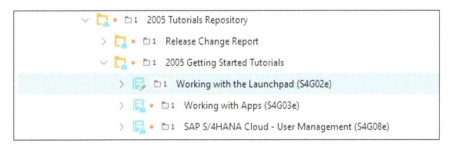

You can now edit and publish this content object in the same way as you would for any other content object.

Reverting to a standard content object

If you subsequently decide that you do not want to keep your customized version of the content object and want to revert to the SAP-provided version, you will need to carry out the following steps:

1. Delete your custom object. This will remove it from your Workarea, but will not automatically revert to the standard version (the way it does in *Manager*).

2. Locate the object in your **Local Trash**, and delete it from there.

3. Go to *Manager*, locate the object in the server trash, and delete it (**Delete Finally**) from there, as well.

★ For some reason, unless you 'revert' the parent, you won't see the deleted object in the *Checkout* dialog box.

4. Back in *Producer*, right-click on the parent object (typically a Group) of the content object you deleted, and select **Revert Object** from the shortcut menu. The following dialog box is displayed:

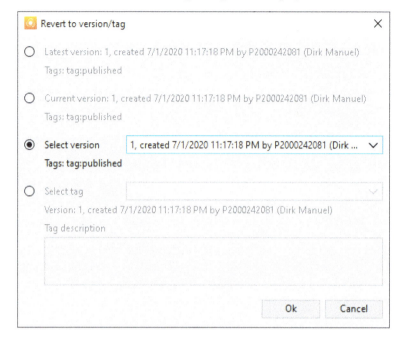

5. Select the last 'good' version, then click **Ok**. The content object you deleted will re-appear in the Workarea (underneath the 'reverted' object)—but will have a black 'question mark' icon in the lower-left of the object icon (see the example below).

6. Select menu option **Server Area | Check Out Objects....** The *Checkout* dialog box is displayed (this may take a while, as it is retrieving a list of all of the content in the underlying standard Workarea).

● In the *Checkout* dialog box, objects that currently exist in your Workarea are shown in black text; objects that are available for downloading/ synchronizing are shown in blue text.

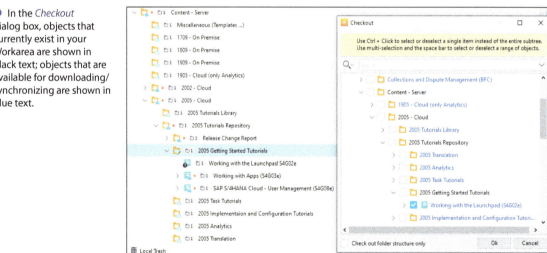

7. Locate and select the content object that you originally extended and then deleted (this is the same object now shown with the 'question mark' icon in your Workarea), and then click **Ok**.

Deleting your **Extended** version of the object automatically restores the standard version from the **Connected** Workarea. You can tell this has happened because the object once again appears with an orange dot to the right of the object icon.

Contextualizing a learning content object

In order for a learning content object to appear in the list of available content (either in the *Learning* page or in the *Learning Center*) it must be tagged with the exact context for the application (and application page, for content on the *Learning* page) with which you want it to be associated. Typically, this learning content will consist of Books. Book Pages, and Simulations, but you can also contextualize Media Objects, which includes video, audio, and image files, as well as PDF files.

✚ The ability to contextualize Media Objects was added in Version 2.3.32.

Suppose we have a Book Page that we want to make available to users when they are using the *Sales Order* screen in our S/4HANA system. Let's add the context for this screen to our Book Page.

To add context to a content object, carry out the steps shown below.

1. In the application (S/4HANA in our example), navigate to the page for which the content object should be proffered as applicable training content, and make sure it is displayed on the screen.

2. Switch to *Producer*. In the *Object Navigation Pane*, select the object you want to use for learning content in Web Assistant. Make sure that you have this object checked out for editing.

3. Click on the **Record** button at the top of the *Object Editor Pane*, and select **Record Web Assistant Context** from the drop-down menu. The *Select Window and Profile* dialog box is displayed.

Record Context

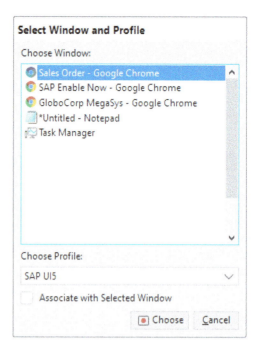

4. In the *Choose Window* list, click on the application from which you want to capture the context. This application window is brought to the front (with the *Select Window and Profile* dialog box still overlaid on top of it), so you can confirm you have selected the correct window.

5. Review the profile selected in the **Choose Profile** field. This should default to the correct recognition profile (especially for SAP systems), but you can change it if necessary.

6. Click on the **Choose** button. The screen context is captured and saved into the **Context** property of the object, and the application details are saved into the properties in the *Web Assistant Context* category. Note that this may take a few moments, and there is no confirmation message to indicate when it is complete.

   For our example, these properties are now as shown below:

7. Don't forget to save the updated object to the server, finish editing it, and then publish your changes (see *Publishing your changes* on page 167).

Now let's go back to our application and confirm that this has worked. If we access the *Sales Order* screen, and display the *Learning* page on the *Carousel*, we will now see the following:

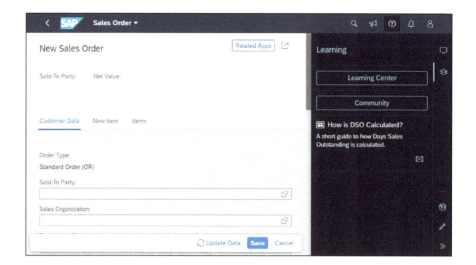

▲ Unlike the **Tile Text** on Help Tiles and Link Tiles the **Tile Text** for learning content Tiles on the *Learning* page cannot be suppressed by setting the parameter `showShortDescription =false`. (This seems like an oversight and may be corrected in a future release.)

Here, you can see that the content object is listed in the *Carousel*, using the object's **Name** as the **Tile Title** and the object's **Short Description** as the **Tile Text**. Success!

This content object will also appear in the *Learning Center*. There, the **Product Name** and **Product Version** are considered (and both must be present/matched), but (obviously) the application page (captured in the **Context** property) is not. This does open an interesting possibility of being able to flag content for inclusion in the *Learning Center* (by maintaining the **Product Name** and **Product Version**) but not on the *Learning* page (by leaving the **Context** blank). You can do this either by capturing all three of these things as described above and then deleting the **Context**, or by manually populating the **Product Name** and **Product Version** field (you can obtain the values to use from the *Context Information* dialog box via the *Carousel*—see on page 61).

Maintaining help context

The help content and learning content displayed via the Web Assistant *Carousel* is context-sensitive. In addition to the **Help Key** (the application page identifier) matching, help content will only be displayed if the **Product Name** and **Product Version** values specified for the application match the **Product Name** and **Product Version** specified in the content object properties. You can see this in the *Help Context Information* dialog box, where the application context values shown in the Requested column, and the returned help object context values are shown in the Available column. An example of this dialog box is shown below, for your reference.

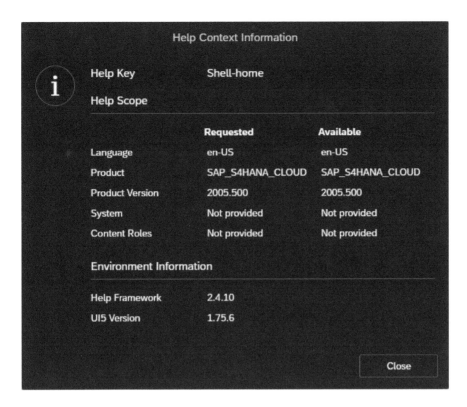

There are two important points to bear in mind here. First, the **Product Version** is considered for context sensitivity. This is important because it means that if your application is updated to a new version, your context-sensitive help and training content may no longer appear, because it refers to the old **Product Version**.

The second thing to understand is that (at least for S/4HANA) the **Requested Product** and **Product Version** are actually retrieved from the Fiori Catalog (for on-premise) or Cloud Plugin (for cloud)—see *Chapter 2, Enabling Web Assistant* for information on these). At first blush, this sounds like good news, as it means that as long as the Fiori Catalog / Cloud Plugin and your content are consistent, your (custom) content will still be displayed. However, there are a couple of problems with this:

- Any new content provided for SAP specifically for the new version will not be displayed, and there is a danger that users could see help content that does not match the application.

- A separate application support team (and not you) may be responsible for the application upgrade, and they are likely to update the Fiori Catalog / Cloud Plugin as part of the application upgrade (it is likely to be on their system update checklist). This is more of a problem, because then the 'requested' context will refer to the new version of the system, but your content will still refer to the old version, so it will not be displayed.

For these reasons, you should coordinate the update of the content with the actual application update. If there is a period when the system is effectively taken down you can replace the context properties at that time. Alternatively, you could choose to add the new product version to your content (so that the content applies to both the current version and the new version) in advance of the application update, and then remove the (now) old version sometime after the application update is complete. In this way, you will minimize the risk of help not being available (or an incorrect version of the help being available) for the application's users.

You may also need to consider your specific Web Assistant 'content model'.

- If you are running a **Standard Content Scenario**, using only SAP's content, then you do not need to make any changes—SAP will automatically update the version number in all of the standard content (both help content and learning content, where applicable).

- If you are running a **Custom Content Scenario** then you will need to update all of your content objects.

- Where things get more complicated is where you are running an **Extended Content Scenario**s and have changed some of the standard SAP content objects. Here, again, SAP will automatically update all of the original standard content in the Connected Workarea. So if you do nothing, your 'extended' versions will now refer to the 'old' version of the application and will therefore no longer be shown in the *Carousel* or in the *Learning Center*. Meanwhile, the standard SAP-provided content will refer to the new version, and will be displayed. The net effect is that all of your custom (extended) content has effectively been removed, reverting to the standard content.

  Here, you have a choice. Your first option is to simply update the Version Number in your extended content to match the application, and this content will then supersede the SAP content again. This is the easiest option but you risk missing out on any changes that SAP may have made to the standard content. The other option is to (re-)extend the new standard version, and re-do your customization in this new extended version. This is more work, but you will benefit from any updates that SAP have made to the standard material.

  There is a strong argument for never actually 'extending' SAP standard content but instead duplicating it, customizing the copy, and then 'hiding' the standard version. Then, whenever there is an application update you can easily compare the 'new' standard version against your 'old' customized version and decide whether you want to revert to the standard version (and then optionally re-extend/re-customize it) or update your custom copy with new information from the standard content.

Updating the context parameters

Thankfully, SAP Enable Now provides an easy way of updating the context in content objects. But first, you should think about how you are going to make your changes.

To update the application context for one or more content objects, carry out the steps shown below:

1. Select the lowest-level Group that contains all of the content objects for which you want to change the application context.

2. Select menu option **Tools | Web Assistant | Context Maintenance**. The *Context Maintenance* dialog box is displayed.

■ This is where it is useful to at least organize your Workarea into folders by application/release—see *Organizing your Workareas* on page 25.

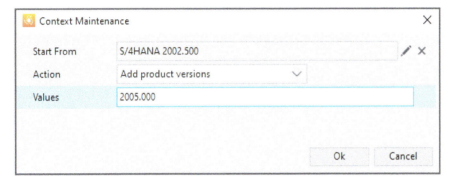

3. The **Start From** field defaults to the Group you selected in Step 1. You can change this if necessary.

4. In the **Action** field, select the type of change you want to make, from the drop-down list. You can choose to add, replace, or delete the existing **Product Name** or **Product Version** (but you need to process them separately).

5. Enter the value you want to add to the existing value, replace the existing value with, or delete from the existing value(s), in the **Values** field. You can specify multiple values as long as you separate them by commas.

6. Click **Ok**.

7. A dialog box is displayed asking you to confirm you want to make the changes.

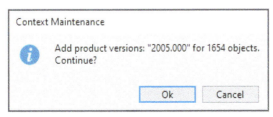

Click **Ok**.

8. If you have included any standard SAP-delivered content in your selection you will be asked if you want to extend the standard content into your Workarea and then update it. You would normally not want to do this.

Click **Yes**.

9. A dialog box is displayed, showing a progress indicator and the number of objects processed. Expand **Show Details** to see information about the objects changed, and the new values. An example of this is shown below:

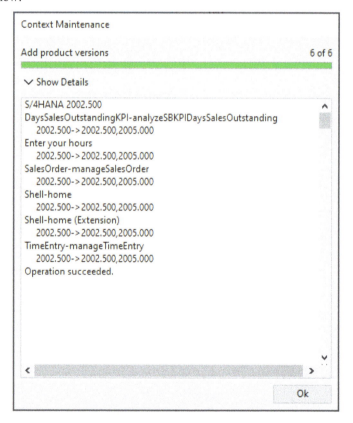

10. Once you see the message `Operation succeeded`, click **Ok** to close the *Context Maintenance* dialog box. (If you do not select **Show Details**, you will know the operation is complete when the progress bar shows **x of y** and x=y.)

11. All of the objects will have been checked out for editing. With the Group you selected in Step 1 still selected, click on the **Show Tree Operations** button, select **Finish Editing All Objects** from the drop-down, and then save/ check in the objects as normal.

Show Tree Operations

Assigning Categories to your learning content

If you have connected a Workarea to the Web Assistant as the *Learning Center* content provider, you can assign Categories to the content objects (Project, Book, or Book Page) in this Workarea, so the user can filter the *Learning Center* to show only content for a specific Category. The image below shows a snippet of the *Learning Center*, showing several Category buttons (the leftmost button is "All"). The Category is shown as a ToolTip when you hover over the button, and the number of learning content objects in the Category is shown in the lower-right corner of the button.

To assign a Category to a content object, carry out the steps shown below.

1. In *Producer*, navigate to and select the content object to which you want to assign a Category. Click on the **Edit** button, to check the object out for editing.

Edit

2. In the *Object Editor Pane*, navigate to the *Learning App Context* category of properties.

➕ The **Weight** and **Duration** properties were discontinued sometime between the 1811 release and the 1911 release of SAP Enable Now.

3. In the **Learning App Category**, enter the Category that should be assigned to the content object. This can be one of:

   ♦ **Tutorial Package**

● The **Tutorial Package** Category was previously named **Learning Package**.

- **Get Started**

- **Processes**

- **Implement**

- **Other**

Note that these are effectively just text labels - it is up to you (or your Master Author) to decide how they will be used, and what type of content you will assign to each Category.

4. Check in the content object, and publish it.

Assigning roles to your learning content

Users have the ability to filter training content in the *Learning Center* by role, by using the drop-down list on the far right of the *Learning Center* screen header. An example of this is shown below.

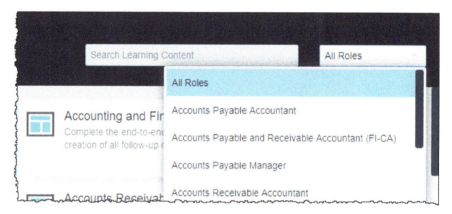

The list of roles is taken from the **Role** property of every applicable learning content object. Here's an example of a Book Page object with the **Customer Service Representative** role assigned to it:

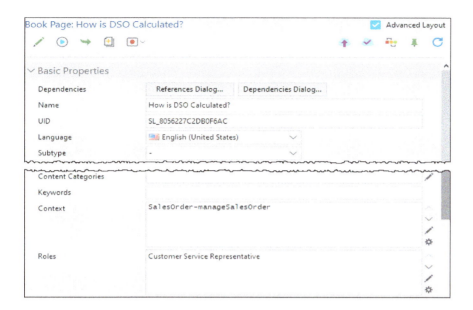

To assign a role to a content object, simply enter the role name in the Roles property field. Note that this field is not validated in any way (there is no pick-list of master roles, like there is for Categories), so you should be careful that you are consistent and spell the role name correctly. (Master Authors may want to create a predefined list in a Text Unit content object and then advise Authors to always copy/paste role names from this list.)

Including standard content in the Trainer

The *Trainer* is the stand-alone browser-based interface that displays all of your (published) training content. You need to provide your users with the URL of the 'entry point' group for the *Trainer*. This entry point must be somewhere under **Root**, but is typically not **Root** itself, as this also contains non user-facing content such as your Toolbox.

As noted in *Where does Web Assistant get its content?* on page 17 you can choose to have the *Trainer* displayed instead of the *Learning Center* when users click on the **Learning** button within the *Carousel*. Although this may be a good idea in order to provide your users with a familiar interface (if they also access the *Trainer* directly) and/or a more easily-navigable interface (if you have a lot of learning content). You should bear in mind that the *Trainer* will only include content that is located under the chosen 'entry point' Group. This means that it specifically will not include any content under **Unsorted**. And as noted earlier in this chapter, all of the standard SAP-provided content is (initially) located under **Unsorted**. This can lead to some unintended confusion, because a user could potentially see a training object on the *Learning* page of the *Carousel*, but then not be able to find this same content object via the **Learning** button because that has been configured to show the *Trainer*, which will not include the **Unsorted** content.

For this reason (and possibly others) you may want to move (or at least 'copy as reference') some or all of the standard SAP-provided content to under your *Trainer* entry point. You may not want to (just) include the entire Group containing the standard content in your *Trainer* entry point Group as the standard content tends to be organized functionally (and not always logically), which may not meet your requirements. That said, there is a good argument for including the entire structure somewhere, so that you never hit the problem of content on the *Learner* page not being in the *Trainer*. So consider including the entire standard content Group at the bottom of your *Trainer* outline, with a name of "Standard content by function" (or something similar - and perhaps with an explanation or disclaimer in the **Description**, just so your users know what they are looking at). You should do this in addition to including any required standard content objects at the relevant points in your overall *Trainer* outline.

Filtering the Trainer

▲ As of the 2005 release of SAP Enable Now, this approach (of filtering the *Trainer*) does not work with a Cloud implementation (although it does with an on-premise implementation). However, I'm leaving this section here, in case SAP rectifies this omission before I publish a second edition of this book.

One final tip. If you are pointing your users to a *Trainer* as the 'Learning App' from a specific application (and the Web Assistant is always for a specific application and version) it makes sense to only have content for that specific application/version included in the *Trainer*. You can achieve this by defining a Filter that includes only this content, and then including this in the URL to the *Trainer* that you specify in the `learningCenterUrl` parameter.

To do this, carry out the steps shown below.

1. Click on the **Filter Workarea** button, and then select **Edit Filters** from the drop-down menu. The *Edit Filter* dialog box is displayed. An example of this is shown below.

Unpublished

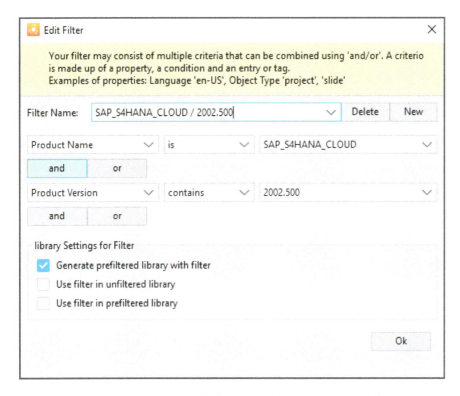

2. Click the **New** button on the far right of the **Filter Name** field.

3. In the leftmost filter field (the **Property**), select **Product Name** from the drop-down list, make sure the middle field (the **Criteria**) specifies **Is**, and enter the application identifier in the rightmost field (the **Value**).

4. Click the **and** button to add a new set of filter fields.

5. Select a **Property** of **Product Version**, leave the **Criteria** as **Is**, and enter a **Value** of the application version.

6. Make sure the **Generate prefiltered library with filter** checkbox is selected.

7. The **Filter Name** field will default based on the specified criteria. You may want to change this to something shorter and more meaningful.

8. Click **Ok** to save your filter.

9. Locate your new filter in the Workarea, under **Resources | Filters**, check it in (**Finish Editing**), and publish it. You will need to do this before you can use it in a URL.

10. Make sure your filter is applied to your Workarea (select it from the **Filter Workarea** button's drop-down list if necessary).

11. Locate the entry point for your *Trainer* (or just use **Root**, if you do not have a specific entry point), and copy its *Start Link* URL from the **Published View** property (or from *Custom Location*, if you use that).

This should include the filter specification in it, as shown in the example below:

```
https://globocorp.enable-now.cloud.sap/pub/
h0b1982dw/index.html?library=libraryFLT_8C5133C7
CD312395.txt&show=group!GR_CAF4B6E41D720F73C
```

This is the URL that you should now specify on the `learningCenterUrl` parameter.

Obtaining links to training content

As we saw in *Chapter 3, Creating Help Content*, you can provide links to training content objects from within the *Carousel*—either via Link Tiles, or by providing a hyperlink within a Bubble (for a Help Tile or a Guided Tour step). If you are providing a hyperlink to an object in the same Workarea, the easiest way to do this is to use the *Web Editor*, but if you have your learning content in a separate Workarea, or you are creating a Link Tile, you will need to obtain the URL of the object. There are a number of ways to obtain the URL for an object, but the most precise way is to use one of the *Start Link* URLs available from *Producer*.

The *Start Links* property category (in the *Object Editor Pane* of *Producer*) contains a number of pre-built links. An example of the *Start Links* category of properties, for a Simulation Project, is shown below.

The **Local Preview** link allows you (and only you) to preview the content (even if it has not been saved to the server, or has not been published). The **Authoring Preview** allows any Authors (or other people who have been granted 'draft' access to the Workarea) to see the content, but Learners will not be able to see it. The **Published View** link is only available once the content object has been published, and typically would be the link that you would use in the Web Assistant (or anywhere else you want to provide a link to the content object). *However*, if you want to track access to the content object (and particularly if you have specified the `trackingUrlWPB` parameter) you should use a URL that contains `/~tag/published/` — which the **Published View** URL does not.

You *could* just manually edit the URL each time, but you will find it easier to use the **Custom Location** link. Typically, this is used to provide the URL of the content object when published to a local web server, but even if you are using a full cloud implementation, you can make use of this parameter. To make this parameter provide a URL that you can use for linking to content objects from the *Carousel*, and that allows tracking, carry out the steps shown below.

1. Take a copy of the **Published View** link for any content object, up to the end of the Workarea specification. (For example, for a cloud implementation this could be `https://globocorp.enable-now.clouds.sap/pub/globotrain/` where `globocorp` is our cloud instance, and `globotrain` is our training Workarea.

2. In the *Object Navigation Pane*, click on the highest-level entry for your Workarea (this has a name of **Workarea: {Workarea ID}**).

3. In the *Object Editor Pane*, locate the **Custom Prefix** property in the *Start Links* category.

4. Paste the link copied from Step 1 into the **Custom Prefix** property, and then add `~tag/published/` to the end of this (so it looks similar to the example in the image above).

Now, the **Custom Location** property for a content object will specify the exact URL you need to use in the Web Assistant. You can copy this URL by clicking on the **Copy Link** button to the right of the URL in the *Property Editor* pane. Note that if you want to link to a specific Simulation mode, you should expand the Simulation Project to display the modes below it, select the required mode, and then copy the **Custom Location** property for this.

Publishing your changes

To publish a content object in a cloud environment, all you need to do is tag it as 'Published'. There are effectively two points at which you can do this. The first point is when you finish editing the content object. This is done as follows:

1. Click on the content object in the Workarea to select it.

2. Click on the **Finish Editing** button. The *Finish editing* dialog box is displayed. Note that this will look slightly different depending on whether a workflow process is assigned to the content object or not. The example below shows a content object that does not have a workflow process assigned to it.

Finish Editing

■ If you want to publish all content objects in a Group, you will find it easier to first select the Group, and then use menu option **Server Workarea | Finish Editing All Objects**, or **Server Workarea | Change Workflow for All Objects** (as appropriate), instead of using the buttons. The remaining steps are the same, but will apply to all objects and not just the single object selected.

3. Next to the **State** label, select the **Publish** checkbox. This is the action that will make the content available—regardless of the **Change Status** setting.

4. Complete the other fields as necessary.

5. Click **Finish Editing**.

If you do not currently have the content object checked out for editing, then you can use the second method of tagging an object as 'Published'. This is as follows:

1. Click on the content object in the Workarea, to select it.

2. Click on the **Change workflow** button. The *Change workflow* dialog box is displayed. Again, note that this may vary slightly depending on whether a workflow process is assigned to the content object. For contrast with the example above, this screenshot (below) is for a content object that *does* have a Workflow Process assigned to it.

Change
Workflow

■ Despite the function name, this method of setting the **Publish** flag via the **Change Workflow** button is not actually limited to only content objects to which a Workflow process has been assigned; you can also use it with any content object to change the **Publish** indicator without checking out the content object.

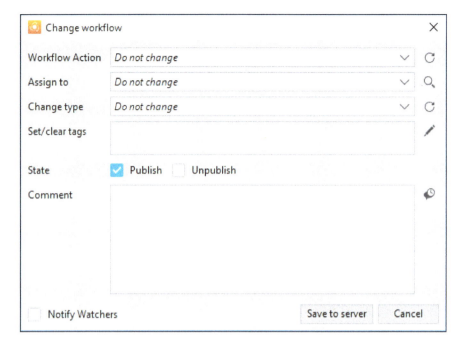

3. Next to the **State** label, select the **Publish** checkbox. This is the action that will make the content available—regardless of the **Workflow Action** (although a Workflow Process can be set up to automatically publish content when the **Status** is changed to a specific value).

4. Complete the other fields as necessary.

   Typically, if you have a Workflow process assigned to the content object, you would select the 'final' **Workflow Action** (for example, "Approved", or "Published"), assign the content object to 'no-one' (select an **Assign to** value of **Unassign**), and change the **Change Type** (typically, to blank, now that the change is complete).

5. Click **Save to server**.

Regardless of which of the above two methods you use, once the **Publish** flag has been set for the content object, it will be visible to your users via the *Carousel* or the *Learning Center* (as applicable)

⚠ Although a content object can technically be published regardless of the object's **Status** (and independently of the Workflow Action if the object has a Workflow process assigned to it) the ability to publish a content object is controlled by permissions. This permission should normally only be given to the role that can progress the object to having a **Status** of **Published** (or whatever your final Workflow step is).

Summary

SAP Enable Now *Producer* is primarily used to create and manage learning content, such as Books, Book Pages, and Simulations (all of which are outside the scope of this book). It is typically not used for creating or editing Web Assistant help content (which is maintained directly via the *Carousel*).

There are a few Web Assistant related activities that are most easily achieved via *Producer*, most notably maintaining context information—for both help content and learning content. You may also choose to use *Producer* to assign Categories and/or Roles to your learning content objects—although you can also do this in *Manager*. As a final tip, if you need to assign **Categories** or **Roles** to multiple content objects, you may find it easier to export (the section of) your Workarea containing those content objects using menu option **Tools | Workarea Structure | Export Structure**, change the values in Microsoft Excel, and then import your changes using menu option **Tools | Workarea Structure | Import Structure**.

7
Localizing Your Content

When a user clicks on the **Help** button to open the *Carousel*, one of the properties that Web Assistant uses to determine if help is available (along with the application, version, and page key) is the language code—which is either specified in the user's profile in the application or selected when they log on (depending upon the application). If content is available in the user's language, then this version is displayed. If content is not available in the user's language, then the English version is displayed, as a fall-back. For this reason, help content is often authored in English first, and then localized into other languages as required.

This chapter describes how to localize *help content*. Learning content is largely localized in the same way, although localizing screenshots in Simulations requires additional steps not covered here.

In this chapter, you will learn:

- How to export help content for submission to a translator
- How to import translated content

Preparing for localization

Before you localize your help content, you should make sure that the primary language version is 100% complete and finalized. Do not waste your time by translating content that may yet change. It is tempting to try to start on the translation as soon as possible, but if you start the translation process and then the original version changes, you will lose too much time and money re-doing the translation, or trying to maintain copies in two (or more) languages.

Translating help text

There are effectively two ways of translating help content text. The first of these is to log into the application using the 'destination' language. This will display the English version of the help content (where no 'destination language' version exists). If you switch to Edit Mode, a new version of the Help Project will be created in the destination language (as the 'current' context). The original version will remain unchanged. You can then over-type the English text with the destination language text. If you are bilingual, this is by far the easiest (and cheapest) option. However, most of us are rarely so fortunate.

This leaves us with the second option, which is to have someone else translate the text for us. Most commonly, this will be a translation service, but it could just as easily be another person in your organization. In either case, it is unlikely that the translator has Author access to SAP Enable Now (and knows how to use it). This means that translation will necessarily involve extracting the text from Enable Now, passing this to a translator to be translated, and then importing the translated text back into Enable Now.

Of these two options, the second option (using a translator) is the most common—and the only one that requires further explanation— so in this chapter, we'll focus solely on this option. As we work through this chapter, we'll use a real-life example. In this example, we are running in an Extended Content Scenario (EXT) for our S//4HANA cloud system. The localization process for a Custom Content Scenario is exactly the same. In a Standard Content Scenario, there is no localization; you just use the standard content, in whatever languages are available.

In our example, we have created one new Tile ("New Users") and have changed the standard "Home" Tile on the *Home* page—all in the English version of our application. Our *Carousel* currently appears as follows:

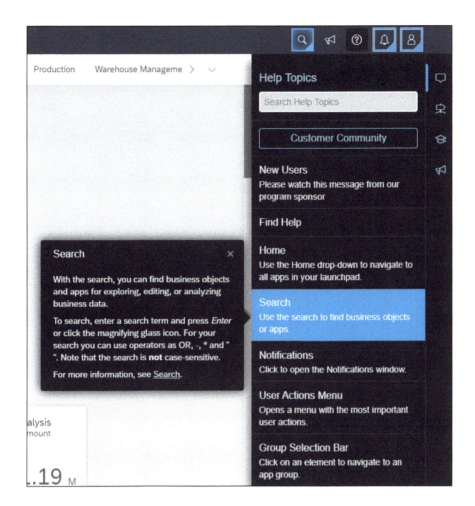

If you display the German version of the *Carousel*, it will appear as shown in the example below. Note that our newly-created Tile ("New Users") is not here, and the "Home" tile shows the standard help (even if you don't know German, you can see that this is shorter than our customized version).

★ For SAP cloud systems, you can quickly switch the application language by adding the parameter **sap-language=XX**, where **XX** is the language code. This is useful for testing without changing your user profile.

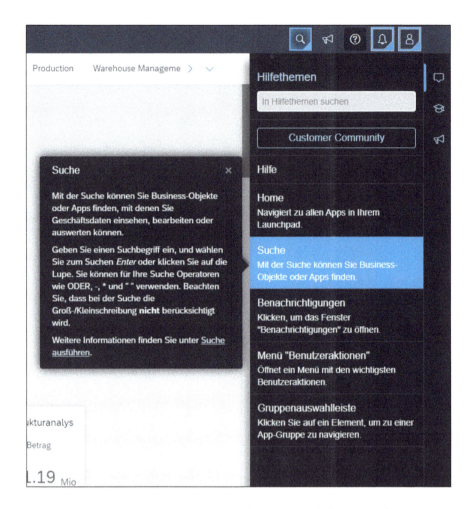

Now let's look at how to translate our English-language help content into German (Language code DE). When we do this, we only want to translate our new Tile, and our customized Tile—all of the other help content we want to just use the standard version, just in German.

Step 1: Duplicate the Help Project(s)

The first thing we need to do is create a new, German version of the Help Project for this application page. To duplicate a Help Project, carry out the steps shown below.

1. In *Producer*, locate the Help Project (Guided Tour or Help Tiles) that you want to translate, and click on it to select it. (You can also select a Group, if you want to translate everything within it.) For information on how to locate a Help Project within Producer, refer to *Locating content in the Workarea* on page 145.

2. Click on the **Duplicate** button (or right-click on the object and select **Duplicate** from the shortcut menu. The *Duplicate* dialog box is displayed.

Duplicate

● If you need to create copies for translating into multiple languages, you may find it easier to use menu option **Tools | Localization | Automated Translation All**.

3. In the **Name** field, select **Keep Original Name**. This is important for Help Tile Projects, because the Project **Name** is the name of the application page. For Guided Tour Projects, the Screen macro is used for context matching, and the **Name** can be translated by the translator.

4. In the **Language** field, select the destination language.

5. In the **Product Version (Web Assistant)** field, select **Keep Original Version**.

6. Select the **Also Save to Server** checkbox.

   If you selected a Group in Step 1, the **Also Save to Server** checkbox is replaced by a **Duplicate subobjects** checkbox, which you should select. This means that there is no option to save the duplicated content objects to the server, so you will need to do this manually.

7. Click **Ok**.

8. Repeat steps 3-7 for all selected objects, if applicable.

9. If you copied a single object, you will be passed into the *Project Editor*. You can exit this immediately (there is nothing you need to do in the *Editor*).

You now have a copy of the Help Project that you can use for translation. If you look in the *Object Navigation Pane* in *Producer*, you will see this:

● To show the language icon alongside the object name, select menu option **View | Workarea Details | Show Language icon**.

Again, it is important to note this is an entirely separate copy of the help content Project, so if the source version changes, you will need to re-copy it and start again.

■ Checking the localized Project at this stage—prior to actual translation—is not done simply out of idle curiosity. It is always advisable to check your work at every stage, and make sure the results are as expected before continuing.

If we now access the German version of our help—without making any other changes—it appears as follows:

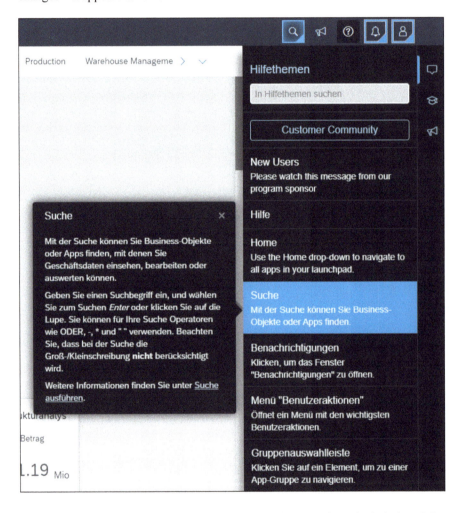

● You can also display the *Help Context Information* dialog box {press *CTRL+SHIFT+I*} and confirm the **Requested Language** and **Available Language** are both as expected.

Here, you can see that our "New Users" Help Tile has now been included, and the "Home Tile" shows our customized text. (This confirms that our new, duplicated Project is being picked up correctly.) Everything else is in German, which shows that it is including the standard version of the help. Now we need to translate the English text.

Step 2: Export the duplicated Help Project(s)

To export your duplicated Help Project(s) in a format that can be sent to the translator, carry out the steps shown below.

1. In the *Object Explorer Pane*, click on the localized Help Project (the one that you created in Step 1), to select it.

   Caution:
   It is important that you select the new, localized Project, and not the original (source-language) Project, because the text in the Project selected here will be overwritten when you import the file after translation.

   ● You can select multiple Simulations or Groups at the same time, if necessary. All localized text for all of the selected content objects will be included in the (single) translation file.

2. Select menu option **Tools | Localization | Export Translation File**. The *Export Translation File* dialog box is displayed.

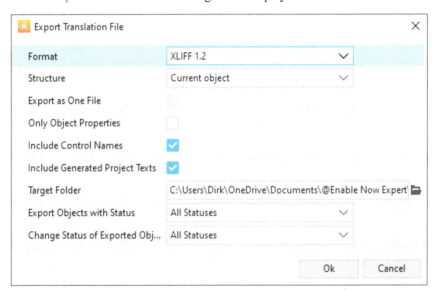

3. In the **Format** field, select the format in which you want the export file to be generated. The following options are available:

   ♦ **XLIFF 1.2**: XLIFF is a specialized XML format that is designed to be imported into a specialized translation software program— typically for initial machine translation followed by manual adjustments.

   ♦ **Microsoft Word**: The text is exported to a Microsoft Word document that can be manually edited by the translator.

   Examples of both of these are shown after these steps.

   If you are not sure which option to use, check with your translator.

4. In the **Structure** field, select whether you want to export only the currently-selected object(s), all of the objects in your Workarea, or all objects inside the selected Group.

5. If your selection includes multiple objects and you want the text for all objects to be included in a single export file, then make sure the **Export as One File** option is selected (this is the default). Otherwise, make sure that this option is not selected, and a separate file will be created for each content object. Generating multiple files is useful if you will divide the translation work between multiple translators or want the translation work to be staggered.

6. Use the button to the right of the **Target Folder** field to navigate to and select the folder into which the exported file should be saved.

■ Of course to do this you will need these Statuses to be defined in your SAP Enable Now installation—typically, in conjunction with a Workflow Process.

7. You can export only Help Projects that have a specific **Status** (for example, only ones that have a **Status** of **Published**), by selecting the required **Status** in the **Export Objects with Status** field.

8. You can also choose to have the **Status** of the exported Projects set to a specific value (for example, **Sent for Translation**) by selecting this **Status** in the **Change Status of Exported Objects** field.

9. Click **Ok**. The objects are exported. Once this has completed, a confirmation dialog box is displayed, giving you the option of opening the exported file, opening the folder it is in, or just closing the dialog box.

You can now pass this file to your translator for translation. Once you receive it back, continue with *Step 3: Importing the translated text* on page 181.

Example of an exported XLIFF file

An example of an XLIFF file generated for localization is shown below. This is purely for information; there are no circumstances under which you would need to manually edit this file type.

Example of an exported Word document

An example of a Microsoft Word document generated for localization is shown below:

★ The text :macro! is followed by the **UID** of the Tile macro in the Project.

```
project!PR_7BREKFBLEX6WJR13FGRFLG12:.caption pt:TEXT
Shell-home (Extension)
project!PR_7BREKFBLEX6WJR13FGRFLG12:.shortdesc rt:html

project!PR_7BREKFBLEX6WJR13FGRFLG12:.description rt:html
This project has been automatically created by the SAP Enable Now Web Assistant.

It is used to extend the following readonly project:
    •  caption: HELP_Shell-home
    •  loio: 354af6ca10fa40109f885c012b2ab415
project!PR_7BREKFBLEX6WJR13FGRFLG12:.keywords pt:TEXT

project!PR_7BREKFBLEX6WJR13FGRFLG12:macro!MAC_67Y8PGCJYJ3AC8RL:.caption pt:TEXT

project!PR_7BREKFBLEX6WJR13FGRFLG12:macro!MAC_67Y8PGCJYJ3AC8RL:.tile_text pt:TEXT_SHORT

project!PR_7BREKFBLEX6WJR13FGRFLG12:macro!MAC_Y7DBJ3WWT6DPP8IG:.caption pt:TEXT
New Users
project!PR_7BREKFBLEX6WJR13FGRFLG12:macro!MAC_Y7DBJ3WWT6DPP8IG:.tile_text pt:TEXT_SHORT
Please watch this message from our program sponsor
project!PR_7BREKFBLEX6WJR13FGRFLG12:macro!MAC_Y7DBJ3WWT6DPP8IG:.bubble_text rt:html

project!PR_7BREKFBLEX6WJR13FGRFLG12:macro!MAC_BEYCWL0BDP8PFJ9C:.caption pt:TEXT

project!PR_7BREKFBLEX6WJR13FGRFLG12:macro!MAC_BEYCWL0BDP8PFJ9C:.tile_text pt:TEXT_SHORT

project!PR_7BREKFBLEX6WJR13FGRFLG12:macro!MAC_BEYCWL0BDP8PFJ9C:.bubble_text rt:html

project!PR_7BREKFBLEX6WJR13FGRFLG12:macro!MAC_DKFAC4CIQGNRQ55F:.caption pt:TEXT

project!PR_7BREKFBLEX6WJR13FGRFLG12:macro!MAC_DKFAC4CIQGNRQ55F:.tile_text pt:TEXT_SHORT
Use the Home drop-down to navigate to all apps in your launchpad.
project!PR_7BREKFBLEX6WJR13FGRFLG12:macro!MAC_DKFAC4CIQGNRQ55F:.bubble_text rt:html
In the shell header, you'll see either Home (when you have the home page displayed) or the title of the current app you
are using. You can click Home to directly open the All My Apps navigation option, or click the app's title to open the
hierarchical navigation menu. The hierarchical navigation menu provides you with several quick actions depending on the
context you are in.
project!PR_7BREKFBLEX6WJR13FGRFLG12:macro!MAC_RRJ7AY5FWPTODQAB:.caption pt:TEXT

project!PR_7BREKFBLEX6WJR13FGRFLG12:macro!MAC_RRJ7AY5FWPTODQAB:.tile_text pt:TEXT_SHORT

project!PR_7BREKFBLEX6WJR13FGRFLG12:macro!MAC_RRJ7AY5FWPTODQAB:.bubble_text rt:html

project!PR_7BREKFBLEX6WJR13FGRFLG12:macro!MAC_33UN0MQLPRCQPJ6X:.caption pt:TEXT

project!PR_7BREKFBLEX6WJR13FGRFLG12:macro!MAC_33UN0MQLPRCQPJ6X:.tile_text pt:TEXT_SHORT

project!PR_7BREKFBLEX6WJR13FGRFLG12:macro!MAC_33UNOMQLPRCQPJ6X:.bubble_text rt:html

project!PR_7BREKFBLEX6WJR13FGRFLG12:macro!MAC_SDK3QEIP8H2G64CI:.caption pt:TEXT
```

★ If you open Project in the *Project Editor* you will see that the corresponding Tile macros are also blank. This is normal.

You will notice that in this example there are a lot of empty sections (red-text 'macro' blocks). These are the macros for the standard Tiles that we have not changed. Do not worry that they are empty (and do not delete them!)—the standard text will still be inserted into them at display time. For translation purposes, you need only concern yourself with 'customized' text (the black text).

Your instructions to the translator should be to "Overtype any black text that follows a 'macro' block with the translated text". Be sure to tell them that they must not change anything else in the file—including any 'code' in square brackets (**[...]**) which denotes formatting, linking, or embedded content.

Step 3: Importing the translated text

Once you receive the file containing the translated text back from the translator, you can load it back into your Workarea. Because the Project and macro identifiers are encoded into the file, SAP Enable Now will automatically know where to place these texts.

To import a translated file (regardless of whether this is in XLIFF or Word format), carry out the steps shown below.

1. Select menu option **Tools | Localization | Import Translation File**. The *Import Translation File* dialog box is displayed.

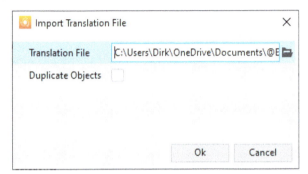

2. Use the button to the left of the **File name** field to navigate to and select the file that contains the translated text.

3. Make sure the **Duplicate Objects** checkbox is not selected. (You have already duplicated the object from the original version.)

4. Click **Ok**. The text is imported, and the text in the duplicated help content Project is overwritten with the new, translated text. Note that there is no confirmation message that this has been done, but for Guided Tour Projects you should see the Project names in the *Project Explorer* change to the local language.

The Help Project(s) will now contain text in the local language. Don't forget to save the Project(s) to the server and finish editing (and set them to **Published**) to make them available (see *Publishing your changes* on page 167).

You will also likely have to finish editing the Group containing the translated Project(s) as this will have been checked out to you when you created the duplicate Project. You might also want to take advantage of the opportunity to reorganize your translated content into language-specific Groups.

If we now go back to our application (still with the language set to German), the *Carousel* will now appear as shown below.

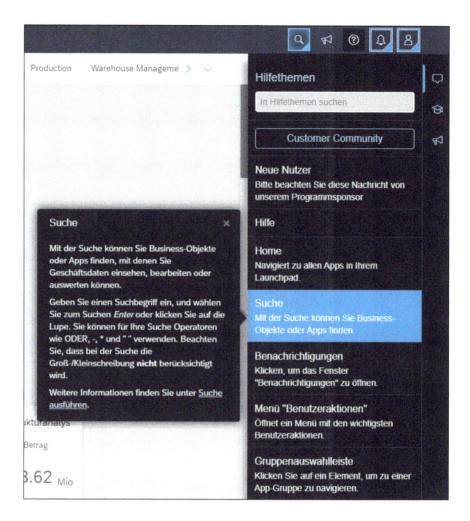

Now, the text in our "New User" Help Tile, and our custom "Home" tile is all in German—and the remaining Tiles still show the standard content in German.

If necessary (now or in the future) you can edit this help content exactly as you would for help content in English (see *Chapter 3, Creating Help Content*).

Summary

Localizing your help content is extremely easy in SAP Enable Now. Help content Projects can be exported in a format suitable for sending to a translator, and then imported back into Enable Now once it has been translated. SAP Enable Now takes care of making sure the translated texts are inserted to the correct content objects in the correct places.

8

Customizing Web Assistant

Although the Web Assistant is largely pre-configured and controlled by the Web Assistant Framework, there are a few things you can do to influence its physical appearance. In this chapter we'll look at these things.

In this chapter, you will learn:

- What pre-defined color schemes are available
- How to change the colors of specific elements
- How to show or hide the **Close** button and the **Minimize** button

Deciding on your Color scheme

Like most aspects of SAP Enable Now, you can exert a fairly detailed level of control over the appearance of the Web Assistant. But before diving down to the lowest level, it is worth checking to see if any of the pre-built color schemes will work for you. Colors are often a matter of personal preference, so unless you have a corporate identity that you *need* to match, it would be advisable to use an existing color scheme if you can. This will also make implementation and ongoing maintenance easier, and is less likely to cause unanticipated problems if there are elements that you cannot change and for which the pre-defined colors clash with your custom scheme.

SAP Enable Now comes several pre-built color schemes, which can be specified via the **themeBase** parameter. An example of each of these is given below, showing the same information so you can easily compare them.

The **default** color scheme provides dark gray tiles with white text, and green highlights and accents. An example of this is shown below:

The **light** color scheme provides light gray tiles with black text, and the same green highlights and accents as the **default** theme. This theme is compatible with the **Quartz Light** theme in Fiori 3. An example of this theme is shown below.

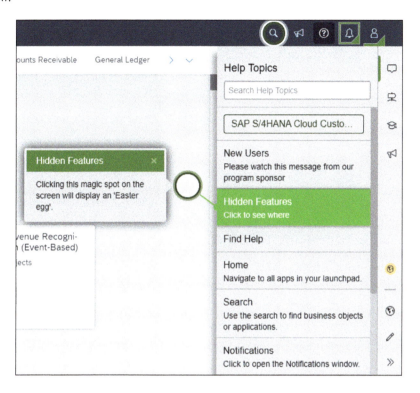

Quartz Light is now the default theme in Fiori 3, so you may want to use this color scheme as the Web Assistant default as well.

The **hcb** color scheme is designed to compliment the **High Contrast Black** theme in Fiori 3. It provides black tiles and white text, and blue highlights and accents. This theme is specifically designed to improve accessibility for visually-impaired users, and is compliant with the *Web Content Accessibility Guidelines 2.1*. An example of this is shown below.

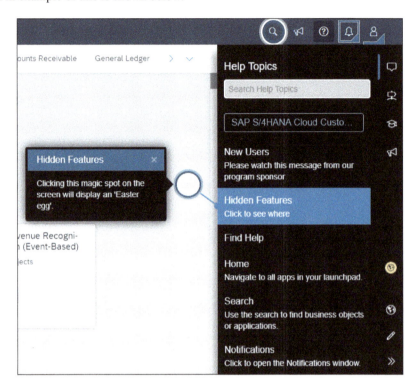

Although not officially documented, there is also a **hcw** ('high contrast white') theme which also complies with the *Web Content Accessibility Guidelines 2.1*. The **hcw** color scheme is designed to compliment the **High Contrast White** theme in Fiori 3.

The **quartz** color scheme is designed to compliment the Fiori 3 **Quartz Dark** theme. It has navy tiles with white text, and lighter-blue highlights and accents. An example of this is shown below.

■ Most of the screenshots used in this book use the **quartz** theme.

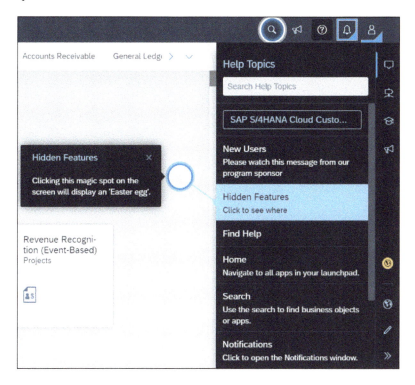

This theme has been designed to be in compliance with the minimal contrast requirements of the *Web Content Accessibility Guidelines 2.1.*

Finally, there is the **sfsf** color scheme. This has been specifically built to complement the SuccessFactors interface, and provides blue tiles with white text, and blue highlights and accents. It also provides a slightly wider *Carousel* (versus the other schemes). An example of the **sfsf** color scheme is shown below.

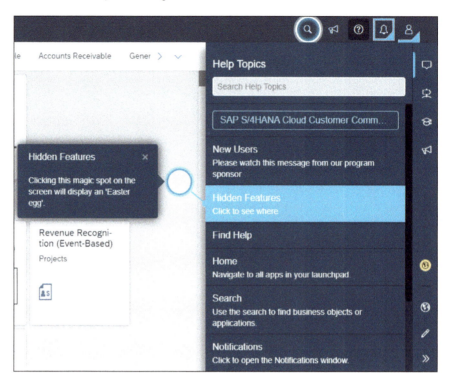

Note that you don't have to use any of these color schemes as-is. You can use individual 'color parameters' (covered below) to override the coloring of any of the customizable elements (as explained in the next section of this chapter). For example, say you like the **sfsf** theme but want green highlights and accents, you can use the following parameters:

```
themeBase=sfsf
accentBg=81,169,0
```

If you do decide to define a custom color scheme, you should plan this out very carefully, taking into account the color scheme of the target application (you would want the Web Assistant color scheme to complement—but stand out from—the application's color scheme). You should also consider the coloring of all applicable Web Assistant elements—especially those elements whose color is derived from (but not taken directly from) the color of other elements, to ensure you don't unwittingly choose incompatible or jarring colors. If possible, use an interface designer who can suggest complimentary and compatible colors. If you don't have the luxury of using such specialist resources, consider using a set of colors identified for a single theme in Microsoft PowerPoint or other application that has predefined color themes.

Customizing the Web Assistant colors

Customizing the colors used in the Web Assistant is surprisingly easy, and doesn't require any knowledge or use of CSS. Instead, the colors used are controlled via parameters, which can be defined in the application (which means that you can define a unique color scheme per application) or in-line in the URL (which is not recommended for a production system, but is a great way of testing color changes if you don't have easy access to the application).

We'll look at three aspects of color customization:

- The *Carousel*, Help Tiles, and Guided Tours
- What's New content
- The *Learning Center*

In each case, we'll identify the elements impacted on one or more screenshots, and follow this up with a table that identifies the parameters that affect these elements. This may require flipping between pages, but this proved to be the most effective way of presenting this information.

The screenshots used in this example were taken with **themeBase=default** specified.

■ You can find an explanation of all color options, along with sample screenshots that isolate the affected elements on http://enablenow.wiki.

The Carousel and Help Tiles

The first set of elements that we will look at are those elements on the *Carousel* itself (including the *Help Stripe*), and elements associated with Help Tiles, Link Tiles, and Guided Tours.

The image below shows a typical instance of the *Carousel*, showing the *Help Topics* page. The alphabetic call-outs are referenced in the table that follows all of the images in this section.

■ An asterisk next to a letter indicates that the color of the identified element is *derived from* the specified color, and does not use the exact color.

This next image shows an example of a Help Tile that has been clicked on, showing the Hotspot, the tether, and the associated Help Bubble. Any elements not directly referenced by a call-out use the same properties as those identified in the main *Carousel* image (above).

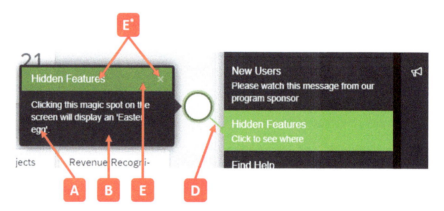

Next, we have a single step from a Guided Tour.

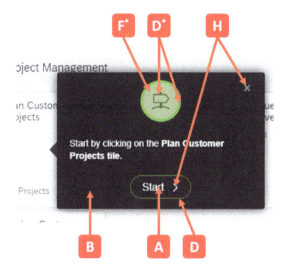

Finally (for this section), we have an example of a pop-up menu. This is taken from Edit Mode. In releases prior to SAP Enable Now cloud release 20.05 there were pop-up menus accessible to users, but this is no longer the case.

Now that we've identified all of the elements that can be customized, let's look at the parameters we need to use to customize them.

ID	Parameter	Elements affected
A	uiFg	• Text in tiles on the *Carousel*
		• Text in Help Bubbles
		• The border around the **Search** field
		• Button text in Guided Tour steps
B	uiBg	• *Carousel* background (including the *Help Stripe*)
		• Help Bubble background
		• *Carousel* scrollbar (derived)

ID	Parameter	Elements affected
C	`accentFg`	• Text in 'selected' Tiles • Text in 'hovered over' Tiles • The 'outer edge' of hotspots • Bubble Titles • Bubble title bar icons (derived)
D	`accentBg`	• Hovered-over Tiles on the *Carousel* • The selected Tile on the *Carousel* (derived) • The 'selected page' indicator on the *Help Stripe* • The hotspot 'highlight' (derived) • The 'tether' line
E	`bubHeadBgCol`	• Background of Bubble header bars
F	`focusFg`	• Text and icons of the element that currently 'has the focus'. Currently only applicable to items on drop-down menus. • The border of any text in a SAP-provided 'link button' (derived) • The background color of Bubble Icons in Guided Tour Steps (derived)
G	`panelHeadlineFg`	• The 'page' title for *Carousel* pages ("Help Content", "Guided Tours, etc.)
H	`iconFg`	• Icons on the *Help Stripe*
I	`focusBg`	The background of the element that currently 'has the focus'. Currently only applicable to items on drop-down menus.

What's New content

Content that appears on the *What's New* page has its own color scheme so it stands out from other content. However, there are significantly less elements for which you can change the color, and most elements use the same colors as the *Help Topics* page.

The following image shows the *What's New* page of the *Carousel*, showing a selected Tile and its associated Bubble.

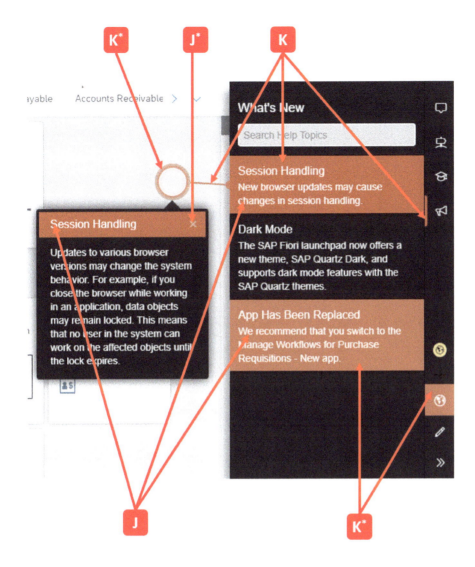

There are only two parameters available for affecting the *What's New* page (effectively replacing the **accentFg** and **accentBg** parameters). These are listed in the table below.

ID	Parameter	Elements affected
J	WNfg	• Text in selected Tiles • Text in 'hovered over' Tiles • The 'inner edge' of hotspots • Bubble Titles • Bubble title bar icons (derived)

▲ **WNBg** also affects Bubble title bar icons, but **WNFg** takes precedence if they are both specified.

ID	Parameter	Elements affected
K	WNBg	• Hovered-over tiles on the *Carousel*
		• Selected tile on the *Carousel* (derived)
		• The 'selected page' indicator on the *Help Stripe*
		• The hotspot 'highlight' (derived)
		• The 'tether' line

The Learning Center

The *Learning Center* generally has its own color scheme, but also uses a couple of the standard *Carousel* colors. The screenshot below shows an example of the standard *Learning Center*, using the parameter **themeBase=default**.

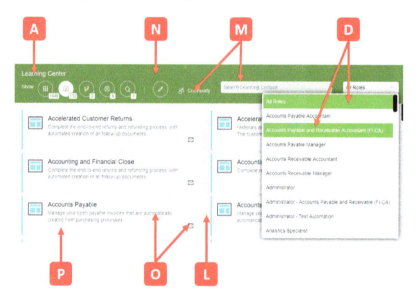

The parameters unique to the *Learning Center* are listed in the table below. Note that there are many elements that (currently) cannot be changed, such as the background of the drop-down list, the color of text in the drop-down list, the accent bar on the leftmost side of the content tiles, and the content type icons.

ID	Parameter	Elements affected
L	LABg	• Background of the screen body area (behind the content tiles)
M	LAHeadFg	• Text and icons in the header bar (except the text "Learning Center", which uses **uiFg**)
		• Border of the **Search** and **Roles** fields
N	LAHeadBg	• Background of the header bar

ID	Parameter	Elements affected
O	LAAssetFg	• All text and icons in the content tiles
P	LAAssetBg	• Background of the content tiles

Customizing the Carousel fonts

You can customize the font family in which text in the *Carousel* (and probably the *Learning Center*) are displayed. This is a little more complicated than changing the colors used, but if you *really* need to change the font, you can do so as explained in this section. If you do change the font you should select a font that is guaranteed to exist on all of your user's workstations (including mobile devices, where applicable).

Locate the local Text Styles

To change the font used by Web Assistant, you need to update the appropriate Text Styles resource for the theme you are using. The theme is specified on the **themebase** parameter (see *Deciding on your Color scheme* on page 183). By default, Web Assistant will use the Text Styles resource included in the Web Assistant Framework. However, copies of these resources can be found in your Workarea, in case you want to customize them. You can find them in the **Resources | Adaptable Resources Group**, with names starting with **Text Styles: Web Assistant**, as shown below:

Text Styles: Web Assistant - Default Theme

Text Styles: Web Assistant - HCB Theme

Text Styles: Web Assistant - Light Theme

Text Styles: Web Assistant - Quartz Theme

Text Styles: Web Assistant - SFSF Theme

These resources are installed by default—with the exception of the SFSF Theme, which for some reason is not. If you want to customize the SFSF Theme, you first need to install it into your Workarea, as follows:

1. Locate SAP Note **2643246 - Use Custom Text Style for Web Assistant in SAP Success Factors**, and download the .dkp file attached to this.

2. In *Producer*, select menu option **Workarea | Import Archive**.

3. Navigate to and select the .dkp file you downloaded in Step 1. The Import Archive dialog box is displayed, showing the contents of the .dkp file.

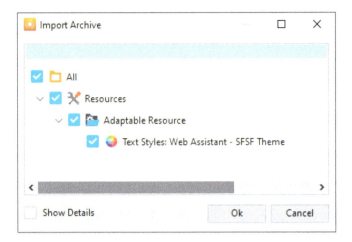

4. Select the checkbox to the left of **All**; this will select the full hierarchy tree all the way down to the one resource in it.

5. Click **Ok** to import the resource.

You can now change the font in this resource as explained in the next section.

Change the font

Locate the Text Styles resource for the theme you want to customize, and then change the font in this as follows:

1. Select the resource and then click on the **Start Editing** button. The resource will be checked out to you.

2. Click on the **Edit Text Styles** button to open the *Text Style Editor*.

Edit Text Styles

3. Make sure the *Defaults* category is shown on the right of the dialog box.

4. In the **Font Family** field, select the required font from the drop-down.

5. Click **Save** to save your changes, then click **Close** to close the dialog box.

6. With the resource still selected, click **Finish Editing** and publish the resource.

Use your custom Text Style

There is one thing left to do: you need to tell SAP Enable Now to use your custom Text Style resource, instead of using the default one in the Web Assistant Framework. Do this by specifying the following Web Assistant parameter:

```
customTextStyles=true
```

You also need to make sure that the **themeBase** parameter specifies the theme that you changed.

Changing the Carousel physical elements

There are a few things that you can do to change some physical aspects of the *Carousel*. In this section, we look at what these are.

Changing the carousel width

The *Carousel* defaults to 280 pixels wide (360 for the **sfsf** color scheme—see *Deciding on your Color scheme* on page 183). You can change this so the *Carousel* takes up more (or less...) space, by using the parameter:

```
verticalW=<n>
```

where <n> is the number of pixels. Although it is tempting to increase the width of the *Carousel* to provide more space for text, bear in mind that the content area of the application page is reduced by the same amount, so the wider the *Carousel*, the less space left for the application. So before you change the width of the *Carousel*, determine the smallest screens used by your users, and ensure that enough space is left for the application.

Note that this width does not include the width of the *Help Stripe*, which takes up a further 42 pixels—and this cannot be changed.

Changing the Tile height

It is not possible to specify the height of tiles in the *Carousel*; they will always be sized automatically—depending upon the amount of **Tile Text** to be displayed—

● This changed in Version 2.4.4. Prior to this, all Help Tiles were the same height, regardless of the amount of text they contained.

to a maximum height that is sufficient to accommodate four lines of **Tile Text**. That said, there are a few things you can do to influence Tile height.

Firstly, you can squeeze more words on a line by enabling hyphenation (otherwise, text will always wrap on word boundaries. To allow hyphenation, add the following parameter:

    hyphenation=true

⚠ This will affect the *Carousel* on all application pages. It is not possible to enable this option for selected pages.

Next, if the problem is that there are too many Help Tiles for the current application page to fit on a single screen, you can choose to display only the **Tile Title** in each Tile, and not the **Tile Text**. To do this, add the following parameter:

    showShortDescription=false

The screenshot below shows an example of the *Carousel* when this parameter is used.

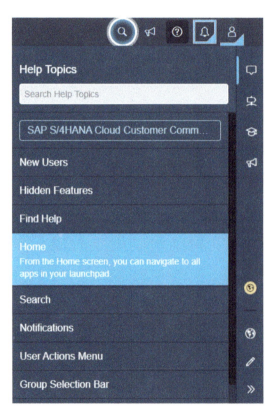

Note that the **Tile Text** is displayed when the user clicks on the Tile in the *Carousel* (as has been done for the **Home** Tile in this example). This, however, is a problem with Link Tiles that do not use the lightbox option, because as soon as the user clicks on the Tile, the target link is opened in a new browser tab, so the **Tile Text** is never displayed (even when you switch back to the application containing the *Carousel*).

Adding or removing navigation buttons

The **Help Content**, **Guided Tours**, and **What's New** buttons will appear on the *Carousel* if there is content of the applicable type available; you cannot change this. The **Learning** button will appear if enabled in configuration (see *Chapter 2, Enabling Web Assistant*), regardless of whether context-sensitive help is available or whether a Learning App has been connected.

There are two further buttons that you can control. These are the **Close** button (which is not shown by default) and the **Minimize** button (which is shown by default). These are identified in the partial screenshot below.

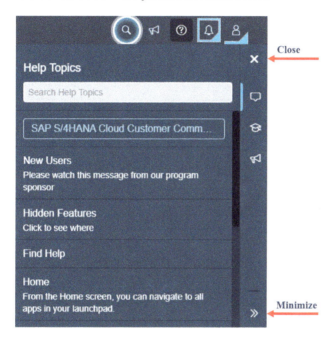

These buttons are controlled by the following parameters:

```
showCloseButton=[true|false]
showMinimizeButton=[true|false]
```

Adding space at the top of the Carousel

There is one last option available regarding the appearance of the *Carousel*. This is the ability to change the amount of space between the top of the application content area and the top of the *Carousel* (including the *Help Stripe*). This only applies to applications not using the Fiori Launchpad (which automatically assigns the required amount of space itself), but can be used to accommodate toolbars or other content that runs from side-to-side of the application page and is not automatically shifted to the left when the *Carousel* is displayed.

● Technically, this would be applications that do not correctly handle the Web Assistant Framework's `onHelpRequireIndent` function.

To manually specify the amount of space to be left at the top of the *Carousel*, use the following parameter:

```
carouselTopSpace=<n>
```

where <n> is an integer between 24 and 60.

Summary

SAP Enable Now provides a large degree of control over the appearance of the Web Assistant *Carousel* and *Help Stripe*. Much of this centers on the ability to change the colors used, but it is also possible to influence the width of the *Carousel*, and the availability (or not) of selected buttons on the *Help Stripe*.

9

Integration with non-SAP Applications

SAP Web Assistant was purpose-built for use with SAP applications, and particularly for those using Fiori or another browser-based interface. Yet at its heart, it is really just a series of utilities that are launched within a browser. This means that you could, technically, integrate it with any web application—as long as you have access to the code of that application so you can perform that integration.

In this chapter, we'll look at how to add Web Assistant functionality to your own browser-based application. This is not a Web Assistant 'look-alike', but full-function official Web Assistant. Which means that you still need Web Assistant installed and running, and need to have a Workarea set up in which to store your help content.

This is probably not for everyone, but if you have Web Assistant installed, and have in-house browser-based applications, you can use Web Assistant with them as well, to provide a consistent EPSS for all your applications—SAP and non-SAP.

In this chapter, you will learn:

- How to attach an existing Web Assistant installation to your own application.
- What changes you will need to make to your application to better support Web Assistant integration.

What you need

In order to use Web Assistant with your own application, you obviously need a fully-licensed, working edition of SAP Enable Now, in which Web Assistant has already been installed. You also obviously need 'Creator' licenses for this (with Cloud, all licenses are effectively Creator licenses). The good news is that you likely have all of this installed and already running for an SAP system.

You may want to consider creating a separate Workarea specifically for your custom application. Remember that all help content is initially stored in the **Unsorted** Group. This can quickly become unmanageable and confusing if you have multiple applications (including SAP systems) saving content to a single Workarea. You should also think carefully about whether you want to use this same Workarea for any associated learning content, want to use your existing Workarea, or want to create an entirely separate one. This is all largely for your own convenience, but bear in mind that you will only be able to include images and videos in your Help Tiles if those images and videos exist in the same Workarea as your help content.

● You can *link to* images and videos located in other Workareas, but to *embed* them as objects via the Web Editor, they need to be in the same Workarea.

The most important requirement, however, is that the screen objects in your application (fields, buttons, and so on—basically anything to which you might want to associate a Help Tile or Guided Tour Hotspot) must have a unique identifier. If your application has not been built this way from the start, it may be a significant effort to go back and add these identifiers to the application code. (See the comments under *Recognition Rules* on page 68.)

A sample Web Application

For the purposes of this chapter, we will use a very simple, one-page browser-based application. Here's what it looks like:

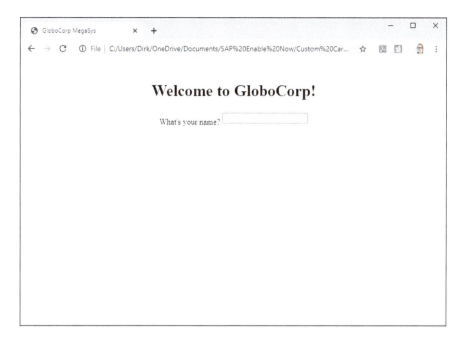

No, it's not pretty (or even functional!) but we will be looking into the HTML code behind this page, and I don't want to clutter it up with extraneous code that is irrelevant for our purposes. This page has one interactive element (the 'Name' field), which is all we need for this 'proof of concept' example.

Building the required code

SAP kindly provide a sample script that you can use as a starting point for Web Assistant integration. Here, I'm using a simplified version of this script, so I can't claim it's an original work—or that I even understand what some of the code does. What I will do is walk you through each section of the code and explain what it does, so you can customize the SAP-provided script yourself. All code in red needs to be changed to match your specific set-up; code in black should be left as-is.

● To obtain a copy of the SAP original code, contact your SAP Customer Engagement Executive (CEE).

All of this code needs to be inserted into the web page header (inside the `<HEAD>...<HEAD>` HTML tags. More technically-savvy readers may want to look at farming the common routines out to a single JavaScript file you can include, but for our purposes we'll keep everything in the same, single file.

The first line of code is probably the most important. This effectively attaches the entire Web Assistant Framework, which does all of the hard work, acting as an interface between our application and the SAP Enable Now Workarea(s).

```
<script src="https://webassistant.enable-now.cloud.
sap/web_assistant/framework/wpb/Help4.js" type="text/
javascript"></script>
```

This is followed by an in-line script which contains all of the rest of the code. Here's the two lines for the script; all of the remaining code sits within this.

```
<script type="text/javascript">
...
</script>
```

The next line creates a global variable that provides access to the Web Assistant instance at run-time (it is set to the Web Assistant instance later in the code).

```
var WebAssistant = null;
```

Next, we have a function that performs all of the initialization. We'll walk through this one block at a time.

```
function setup_web_assistant() {
  var btn = document.createElement("BUTTON");
  btn.id = "GloboHelp";
```

This code (above) is important, and creates our **Help** button (the equivalent of the (?) button in an SAP system). Pay close attention to the `btn.id` value - you will need to use this exact same name elsewhere in your code.

Next, we perform some initialization:

```
var oHelp = Help4.init({
  type: 'generic',
  product: "GloboCorp_MegaSys",
  version: "1",
  language: 'en-US',
  buttonId: 'GloboHelp',
```

Here (above) we again have the **Help** button identifier. We also have the product name and version information, which is used for the context-sensitivity, and we have a language specification.

The next set of parameters are all standard Web Assistant parameters. These are all described in *Chapter A, Web Assistant Parameters* if you need more information.

```
    serviceLayerVersion: 'WPB',
    resourceUrl: 'https://webassistant.enable-now.cloud.
sap/web_assistant/framework/',
    dataUrlWPB: 'https://globocorp.enable-now.cloud.sap/
wa/globohelp/',
    learningAppBackendUrl: 'https://globocorp.enable-now.
cloud.sap/',
    learningAppWorkspace: 'globotrain',
    noHelpMode: 'carousel',
    rtl: 'false',
    mobile: 'false',
    editor: false,
    multipage: true,
    showWhatsNew: true,
    themeBase: 'default',
```

The key parameters here are `dataUrlWPB` which specifies the Workarea in which the custom help you create will be stored, and the `learningAppBackendUrl` and `learningAppWorkspace` parameters which specify the Workarea in which the learning content is located. (As noted before, these can be the same Workarea.)

You can also include additional parameters in this section (for example to customize the *Carousel* colors, as explained in *Chapter 8, Customizing Web Assistant*) as necessary.

Next—and still within the `var oHelp = Help4.init ({...})` block—we have a set of functions that are called in response to events in the Web Assistant Framework. Mostly, these are used to change the appearance of the Help button, and/or write messages to the browser console to explain what has happened (these console statements aren't necessary for Web Assistant to work, but you will find them invaluable for troubleshooting during your initial implementation). The 'events' are highlighted in bold for your ease of reference. A full list of all available events is given at the end of the code snippet.

★ To display the Chrome browser console, press *F12* and then select the *Console* tab.

```
onHelpBusy: function(busy) {
    console.log("help busy " + (busy ? "true" :
"false"));
    style.visibility = busy ? "visible" : "hidden";
    document.getElementById(btn.id).src = busy ?
"helpWarning.png" : "helpActive.png";
    },
onHelpAvailable: function(bAvailable) {
    console.log("help available " + (bAvailable ?
"true" : "false"));
    document.getElementById(btn.id).src = bAvailable ?
"helpActive.png" : "helpInactive.png";
    },
onHelpMinimized: function(bMinimized) {
    console.log("help minimized " + (bMinimized ?
"true" : "false"));
    document.getElementById(btn.id).src = bMinimized ?
"helpMinimized.png" : "helpActive.png";
    },
onHelpActive: function (bActive) {
    console.log("help active " + (bActive ? "true" :
"false"));
    document.getElementById(btn.id).src = bActive ?
"helpActive.png" : "helpNormal.png";
    },
onHelpMode: function (mode) {
    console.log("help mode " + mode);
    },
onHelpCarousel: function (bCarousel) {
    console.log("help carousel " + (bCarousel ? "true"
: "false"));
    },
```

```
    onHelpRequireIndent: function (bIndent, indentWidth)
{
    console.log("help indent " + (bIndent ? "true" :
"false"));
        if (bIndent) {
        document.documentElement.style.marginRight =
indentWidth + "px";
        } else {
        document.documentElement.style.marginRight = "0";
        }
    },
```

The following table provides a list of all available functions and explains the circumstances under which they are invoked.

Function	Purpose
onHelpBusy	Called when the Web Assistant is busy loading the help content. Parameters: • isBusy=[True|False]
onHelpAvailable	Called when content is available for the current application page. Parameters: • contentAvailable=[True|False]
onHelpMinimized	Called when the *Carousel* is minimized (and only the Help Stripe is displayed). Parameters: • isMinimized=[True|False]
onHelpActive	Called when Web Assistant is opened or closed (via the **Help** button). Parameters: • isActive=[True|False]
onHelpMode	Called whenever the Web Assistant 'mode' changes. Parameters: • helpMode=[help|helpEdit|tour|tourEdit]
onHelpCarousel	Can be called to determine whether the *Carousel* is displayed or hidden (for example, it is hidden during Guided Tour playback). Parameters: • hasCarousel=[True|False]

Function	Purpose
onHelpRequireIndent	Called when the *Carousel* 'slides out', and can be used to reduce the application's width to accommodate the *Carousel*.
	Parameters:
	• bIndent=[True|False]
	• indentWidth={*number of pixels*}
getEnvironmentInfo	No idea. A comment in SAP's code states "Web Assistant features a configuration dialog available for editors option menu. This function allows to add own values to that dialog, e.g. Framework version" if that's any help.

The only thing you should need to change in the functions is the references to the graphics for the **Help** button. For this simple example, we have used the following graphic files:

helpNormal.png

helpInactive.png

helpActive.png

helpMinimized.png

helpWarning.png

The next block of code is used to determine what recognition modes can be used for identifying screen elements in our application for Hotspot assignment. You should not change any of this code.

```
selector: {
  blacklist: [],
  rules: ['DataAttrSelector', 'DomIdSelector'],
  selectors: {
    DomIdSelector: {
      safe: true,
      getSelector: function (elem) {
        return elem.id || null;
      },
      getElement: function (selector) {
        return document.getElementById(selector);
      }
    }
  }
}
```

Finally, we have the end of the initialization function.

```
}); // end of init function call
```

After this, we have code that is executed only if initialization was successful (`oHelp` was instantiated):

```
if (oHelp) {
  oHelp.setAppName("GloboCorp-home");
  btn.onclick = oHelp.toggle.bind(oHelp);
WebAssistant = oHelp;
  }
}
</script>
```

The `setAppName` statement is where we specify the name of the application page that we are creating help for. It is important that this value (in red) is unique for every page (screen) of our application, as this will be used to name the help content Project(s) that we create, which then determines which application page this help will be displayed on.

So far so good. That's the end of the JavaScript (and the end of the HTML `<HEAD>` element). Next, we have our actual code of our application web page. For our simple example application, this is:

```
<BODY onload="javascript:setup_web_assistant();">
<p style="text-align:right;"><a
href="javascript:WebAssistant.toggle();"><img
id="GloboHelp" src="helpNormal.png" style="border:0"></
a></p>
<h1 style="text-align:center;">Welcome to GloboCorp!</h1>
<table align="center">
<tr>
<td>What's your name?</td>
<td><form><input name="Name" type="text"
id="gchUserName"></form></td>
</tr>
</table>
</BODY>
```

Here, the following code is of particular importance:

- The `onload` statement sets up the Web Assistant for use, as soon as the application page is displayed. Without this, nothing works.

- The `<img>` statement displays our **Help** button, and the `id` property on this must match the identifier of the button as specified (twice) in the JavaScript code. This image has a link around it (`<A href=...`) which calls the `WebAssistant.toggle` routine whenever the button is clicked. This routine is located in the Web Assistant Framework, which then, along with performing the actual Web Assistant functions, calls the various `onHelp*` functions in our code.

- We have an `id` property on the input field screen element. This is critical. The `id` is used by the Recognition Rule to uniquely identify this object so we can assign a Hotspot to it. Ideally, every single element in your application should have a unique `id` specified for it.

And that is all of the code! Relatively simple, really.

Testing the result

Now let's see how this looks in action. First, here's our application page once this code has been added to it:

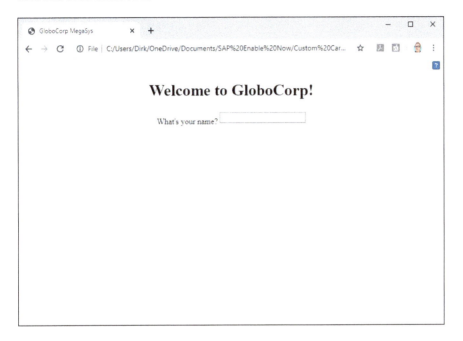

We now have a **Help** button displayed on the upper-right of the screen, using the `helpNormal.png` image. Clicking on this opens up the *Carousel*, as expected—and the screen content has been resized so it is not hidden by the *Carousel*, just like with Fiori:

In the interests of brevity I've omitted the initial screen you'll see stating **Help Content Not Available** (there's an example of this on page *60)* and have entered Edit Mode.

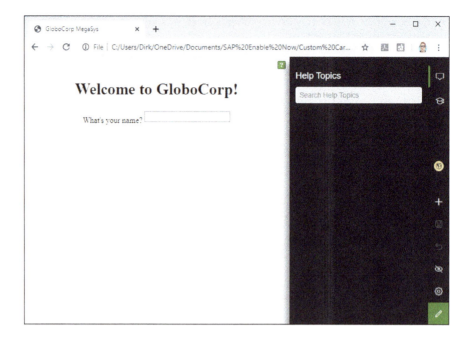

Success! Now let's add some help content to this. We'll add a Help Tile, and then attempt to anchor this to the input field on the application screen.

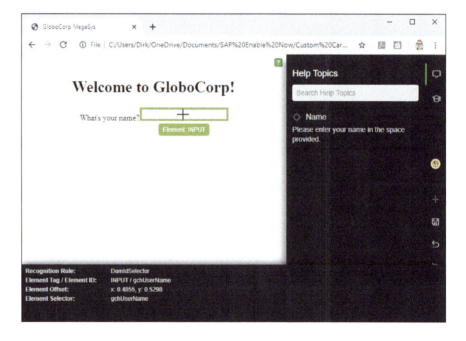

Here, you can see that the screen element in our application is being correctly identified as a suitable candidate for Hotspot assignment. Also, for the sake of complete clarity, this screenshot was captured with the *Recognition Information*

panel displayed, in which you can see that the Element ID is `gchUserName`, which matches exactly what we specified in our application code.

Now let's look at how this appears during playback, to the users of our application:

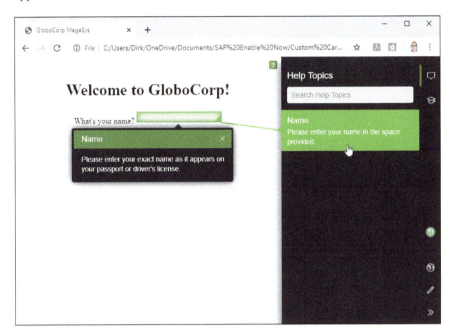

Again, everything here works perfectly. So now we have a fully-functioning (and full-function) Web Assistant running against our own, non-SAP application!

To close the loop on all of this, let's take a quick look at what is saved to SAP Enable Now. The Projects containing our new help content are saved in the Workarea specified by the `dataUrlWPB` parameter. If we go and look in this in Manager, we'll now see something similar to the following:

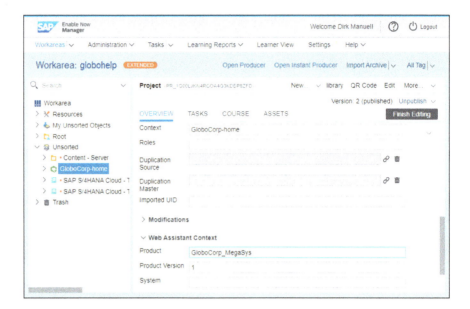

In case you're wondering why the screen name variable is named AppName, remember that Web Assistant was originally built for Fiori, where functions are referred to as 'apps'.

As always, the help content is saved to the **Unsorted** folder, and each Project has the same name as the AppName (which is actually the screen name). This screen name is also stored in the **Context** property of the Help Project. More significantly, you can see that the **Product** and **Product Version** in the *Web Assistant* category have been filled in correctly—this is what gives us the context-sensitivity in Web Assistant.

You can see the same context information by displaying the *Context Information* panel in the application (by clicking on the Edit Mode **Options** button and selecting **Show Context Information** from the pop-up menu, or by pressing *CTRL*+*SHIFT*+*I* [even in Display Mode]). An example of this panel is shown below.

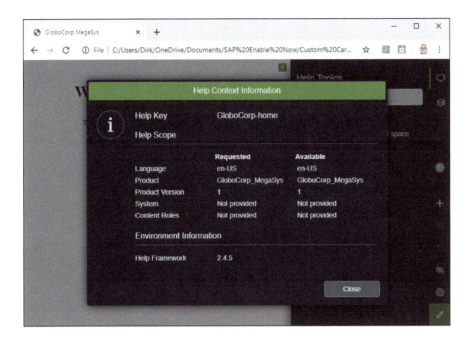

Summary

In this chapter, you have seen how to implement Web Assistant as the EPSS for non-SAP applications—as long as you have the ability to access the source code for these applications, so that you can insert a **Help** button and the JavaScript code necessary to call the Web Assistant functionality.

For additional information on updating your browser based applications to integrate with Web Assistant, consider taking the SAP course *SAP Enable Now: Basic Training for Master Authors*.

A

Web Assistant Parameters

This appendix lists all known Web Assistant parameters. These can be specified in the application (for which help is being provided) or in-line in the URL. If specified in a URL, the parameter should be prefixed by "help-". Of the two, the URL in-line parameter takes priority—which is very useful for testing.

All parameters (and their values) are case-sensitive and typically use camelCase—where each 'word'—except the first—has a capital letter, and the rest is lowercase.

 In Chrome, you can use the Console command **Help4.getShell()._params** to display a list of all parameters and their current values—regardless of whether these were set in the application or in the URL.

accentBg   *See page 190*

Used to specify the background color for the following elements:

- Hovered-over tiles on the Carousel (except for on the What's New page, where **WNBg** is used instead)
- The 'selected tab' indicator on the *Help Stripe*
- The Hotspot 'highlight'
- The Hotspot 'tether' line
- The border and text in *Carousel* buttons (derived)

Specified as:

```
accentBg={R,G,B}
```

where {R,G,B} are the comma-separated decimal RGB values of the chosen color.

accentFg   *See page 190*

Used to specify the background color for the following elements:

- Text and icons for hovered-over tiles on the *Carousel* (except for on the *What's New* page, where **WNFg** is used instead)
- The 'outer edge' of Hotspots (except the current Hotspot)
- Bubble Titles

Specified as:

```
accentFg={R,G,B}
```

where {R,G,B} are the comma-separated decimal RGB values of the chosen color.

✛ **activatePhone** was added in Version 2.4.2.

activatePhone

If set to **true**, Web Assistant is activated for use on mobile devices. Effectively, this causes the **Help** option (button and text) to be included on the drop-down 'more' menu. Selecting **Help** will then display the *Carousel* as normal. This can take up a good portion of the screen (in landscape mode), so if your users will predominantly be using mobile devices, you may also want to use the **verticalW** parameter to reduce its width.

Specified as:

```
activatePhone=[true|false]
```

autoStartTour

Used to specify a Guided Tour that should be launched automatically when the user logs on to the application. This will only take effect if the applies to the first screen the user sees when they first log on (so is best used for the *Home* screen, or equivalent).

Specified as:

```
autoStartTour={UID of Web Assistant Guided Tour}
```

This parameter can also be specified as **tour=**, although this may be a hold-over from an earlier implementation and may be deprecated.

bubHeadBgCol   *See page 190*

Used to specify the background color of the 'header bar' in help bubbles, including Context Help bubbles and Guided Tour step bubbles.

Specified as:

```
bubHeadBgCol={R,G,B}
```

where {R,G,B} are the comma-separated decimal RGB values of the chosen color.

buttonLocation

This parameter (in theory) specifies the position of the **Help** button within then user interface. Currently there is only one option—**head**—so this is probably for future expansion (possibly for applications that already have other 'help' buttons in the header—such as Ariba).

Specified as:

```
buttonLocation=head
```

carouselTopSpace

See page 199

✚ carouselTopSpace was added in Version 2.4.5.

This property can be used to reserve a specific number of pixels between where the top of the *Carousel* would normally appear (typically, below the toolbar or header) and where you want it to appear. This is useful for applications that include additional information immediately below the header/toolbar that should not be obscured by the *Carousel*.

Specified as:

```
carouselTopSpace={nn}
```

where {nn} is a number between 24 and 60.

customTextStyles

See page 195

If this parameter is set to **true** then the text styles used in the Web Assistant are taken from the relevant Text Styles resource in the Workarea, depending on the value of the **themeBase** parameter.

Specified as:

```
customTextStyles=[true|false]
```

The Text Styles are **Default**, **Light**, **HCB**, **SFSF**, and **Quartz**. They can be found in the Workarea under **Resources | Adaptable Resources** and can be customized as required.

dataUrlWPB

See page 25

This parameter is used to specify the source of your custom Web Assistant help content (WPB or EXT scenarios).

Specified as:

```
dataUrlWPB={url}
```

where {url} depends upon the setting of the **serviceLayerVersion** parameter as follows:

serviceLayerVersion	dataUrlWPB
UACP	https://cp.hana.ondemand.com
EXT	https://cp.hana.ondemand.com
WPB	{Your Manager URL incl. Workarea ID}

dataUrlWPB2

See page 25

This parameter is used to specify the URL of the Workarea in which your custom Web Assistant help content is located, if you are running an Extended Content Scenario (both SAP standard content and custom content is used) - in which case the **dataUrlWPB** parameter already specifies the SAP default content URL.

Specified as:

    dataUrlWPB2={Your Manager URL incl. Workarea ID}

disableManualLogin

✚ **disableManualLogin** was added in Version 2.3.33.

If a user (trying to display Web Assistant help) cannot be authenticated via SSO, by default they will be presented with a manual login screen. If this parameter is set to **true** then the manual login screen is not displayed and the SAML panel (or window) is simply closed. If a user is not authenticated the results are as follows (after the SAML authentication window is closed):

- If the **serviceLayerVersion** parameter is set to **UACP** or **WPB** then the user will see only the SAP standard content in the Web Assistant.
- If the **serviceLayerVersion** parameter is set to **EXT** then the **Help** button is hidden and the user will not be able to access Web Assistant at all.

Specified as:

    disableManualLogin=[true|false]

editor

See page 57

If set to **true**, the editor is enabled for the Web Assistant; users will see the **Edit** button at the bottom of the *Help Stripe*. Note that this does not necessarily mean that the users can create or edit content; only users that have write permission to the Workarea will be able to.

Specified as:

    editor=[true|false]

focusBg

This property is used to specify the background color of the element that currently 'has the focus'—for example, the active selection on sub-menus. There are only 'sub-menus' on the *Carousel* in Edit Mode.

Specified as:

    focusBg={R,G,B}

where {R,G,B} are the comma-separated decimal RGB values of the chosen color.

focusFg

See page 190

This property is used to specify the color of text and icons for the active selection on *Carousel* sub-menus. Note that there are only 'sub-menus' on the *Carousel* in Edit Mode.

Specified as:

    focusFg={R,G,B}

where {R,G,B} are the comma-separated decimal RGB values of the chosen color.

hyphenation

See page 197

hyphenation was added in Version 2.3.32.

If this parameter is set to **true** then the description in Help Tiles may be hyphenated if necessary; otherwise all words are un-hyphenated and will flow to the next line as necessary.

Specified as:

    hyphenation=[true|false]

iconFg

See page 190

This property is used to specify the color of icons on the *Help Stripe*.

Specified as:

    iconFg={R,G,B}

where {R,G,B} are the comma-separated decimal RGB values of the chosen color.

infoBarTimeout

This parameter specifies the number of seconds for which informational messages will be displayed at the top of the screen before being

SAP ENABLE NOW WEB ASSISTANT | 219

dismissed. These messages are typically seen by Authors during content maintenance, such as **Save successful**, and so on.

Specified as:

```
infoBarTimeout={seconds}
```

where {seconds} is a positive integer.

infoBarTimeoutWhatsNew   *See page 94*

If this parameter is specified then a 'What's New' message (**We have added some great new features. Click here to find out more.**) will be displayed at the top of the screen the first time a user accesses the screen after logging on. Clicking on this message opens the *Carousel* and displays the *What's New* page.

Specified as:

```
infoBarTimeoutWhatsNew={seconds}
```

where {seconds} is a positive integer.

LAAssetBg   *See page 194*

Used to specify the background color of object 'tiles' in the *Learning Center*.

Specified as:

```
LAAssetBg={R,G,B}
```

where {R,G,B} are the comma-separated decimal RGB values of the chosen color.

LAAssetFg   *See page 194*

Used to specify the color of text and icons on object 'tiles' in the *Learning Center*.

Specified as:

```
LAAssetFg={R,G,B}
```

where {R,G,B} are the comma-separated decimal RGB values of the chosen color.

LABg

See page 194

Used to specify the background color of the main *Learning Center* page (excluding the screen header, which is changed via the **LAHeadBg** parameter).

Specified as:

    LABg={R,G,B}

where {R,G,B} are the comma-separated decimal RGB values of the chosen color.

LACommunityUrl

This property is used to specify the URL of the website that should be opened when the user clicks on the **Community** button in the *Learning* page of the *Carousel* or in the *Learning Center*. Typically, you would do this to direct users to a user community for the application, such as a SAP JAM or Yammer site.

Specified as:

    LACommunityUrl={URL}

LAHeadBg

See page 190

Used to specify the background color of the *Learning Center* screen header.

Specified as:

    LAHeadBg={R,G,B}

where {R,G,B} are the comma-separated decimal RGB values of the chosen color.

LAFeedback

See page 15

LAFeedback was added in Version 2.3.10.

This parameter can be used to suppress the display of the **Learner Feedback** icon in learning content tiles in on the *Learning* page in the *Carousel* and in the *Learning Center*.

Specified as:

    LAFeedback=[true|false]

LAHeadFg

See page 194

Used to specify the color of text and icons on the screen header in the *Learning Center*. Note that the heading "Learning Center" is apparently not affected by this property.

Specified as:

```
LAHeadFg={R,G,B}
```

where {R,G,B} are the comma-separated decimal RGB values of the chosen color.

learningAppBackendUrl *See page 25*

This parameter specifies the URL of the SAP Enable Now *Manager* that contains the content that is to be displayed within the 'Learning App' (*Learning* page within the *Carousel* or the *Learning Center*).

Specified as:

```
learningAppBackendUrl={URL}
```

Note that you do not specify the Workarea in the URL. The Workarea is specified via the **learningAppWorkspace** parameter.

learningAppWorkspace *See page 25*

This parameter specifies the ID of the Workarea that contains the content that is to be displayed within the 'Learning App' (*Learning* page within the *Carousel* or the *Learning Center*).

Specified as:

```
learningAppWorkspace={Workarea ID}
```

➕ `learningCenterUrl` was added in Version 2.3.31.

learningCenterUrl

By default, clicking on the **Learning Center** button on the *Learning* page of the *Carousel* will launch the *Learning Center* (showing content taken from the Workarea specified by the **learningAppBackendUrl** and **learningAppWorkspace** parameters). The **learningCenterUrl** parameter can be used to specify another destination for the **Learning Center** button. This was originally implemented to allow the standard SAP Enable Now *Trainer* to be displayed in place of the *Learning Center*, using a more logical (albeit dated) interface users are likely already familiar with. Technically, it can be used to specify any target, such as a non-SAP Enable Now repository, SAP Learning Hub, a SuccessFactors implementation, and so on.

Note that even if this parameter is specified, the 'context-specific' help on the *Learning* page of the *Carousel* will still be taken from the SAP Enable Now Workarea specified in the **learningAppBackendUrl** and **learningAppWorkspace** parameters.

Specified as:

```
learningCenterUrl={URL}
```

newWindowSAML

See page 34

✚ newWindowSAML was added in Version 2.3.32.

By default, SAP Enable Now attempts to perform authentication from within an iFrame in the browser. Some authentication providers (most notably Microsoft Azure and Okta) do not permit this. To cater for these authentication providers, if this parameter is set to true then a new browser window is opened specifically to perform authentication. This window is automatically closed once authentication has been carried out.

Some browsers block the opening of new windows for security reasons, so you may also need to change the browser settings to 'allow pop-ups'.

Specified as:

```
newWindowSAML=[true|false]
```

noHelpMode

When a user navigates to an application page, SAP Enable Now checks the help content Workarea to see if help is available for that specific page. The **noHelpMode** parameter determines what happens if no help is available (technically, if the **onHelpAvailable** function is triggered with a value of **false**).

If you use a parameter of **readCatalogue=false** then this prevents the help content check from being made at the time the page is loaded, and defers it until the user clicks on the Help button. (This is often done in SuccessFactors to prevent an additional authorization check being performed when the user first logs on.) This is obviously a problem if the Help button is not displayed, as the user has no way of calling up the help (actually, they can press *F1* but there is no indication that they can do this). Therefore, if you use **readCatalogue=false** you should also set **noHelpMode** to **nothing** or **carousel** (of the two, **carousel** is recommended).

Specified as:

```
noHelpMode=[hidebutton|nothing|carousel]
```

These values have the following effects:

Value	Effect
hidebutton	The Help button is hidden when no help is available.

Value	Effect
nothing	The **Help** button is displayed, even if no help is available. Clicking on it will display the "No help available" dialog box, which can be confusing for users, so this is not recommended.
carousel	The **Help** button is displayed, even if not help is available. Clicking on it will open the *Carousel*, with either the *Learning* page displayed (if configured to display), or an empty *Help Topics* page.

openImmediately

This parameter can be used to force Web Assistant to automatically be opened as soon as the user logs on to the application. (The user does not need to click on the **Help** button.)

Specified as:

```
openImmediately=[full|minimized]
```

These values have the following effects:

Value	Effect
full	The full *Carousel* (and *Help Stripe*) is displayed.
minimized	Only the *Help Stripe* is displayed.

panelHeadlineFg

See page 190

Used to specify the color of the *Carousel* 'page heading' ("Help Topics", "Guided Tours", "Learning", or "What's New", depending upon the page).

Specified as:

```
panelHeadlineFg={R,G,B}
```

where {R,G,B} are the comma-separated decimal RGB values of the chosen color.

readCatalogue

This parameter is specific to SuccessFactors. If set to **true**, it suppresses the (SAP Enable Now) user authentication check (which usually occurs as soon as the user logs on to the system) until the user clicks on the Help button (and actually needs the SAP Enable Now help).

Specified as:

```
readCatalogue=[true|false]
```

resourceUrl

This parameter specifies the location of the Web Assistant resources, such as CSS, fonts, and so on. This should always be set to the same value.

Specified as:

```
resourceUrl=resources/sap/dfa/help
```

saml2

If specified, this parameter will bypass SSO authentication, and prompt the user to manually log in. This should only be used for troubleshooting purposes.

Specified as:

```
saml2=Disabled
```

serviceLayerVersion See page 26

This property is used to determine the source of the help content displayed in the *Carousel*.

Specified as:

```
serviceLayerVersion=[UACP|WPB|EXT]
```

These values have the following effects:

Value	Effect
UACP	Only the default SAP-provided content is used. This is the Standard Content Scenario.
WPB	Only customer-created content is used. This is the Custom Content Scenario.
EXT	Customer-created content will be shown where it exists, otherwise the SAP-provided content will be used. This is the Extended Content Scenario.

showCloseButton See page 199

If this parameter is set to **true** then a **Close** button is shown at the top of the *Help Stripe*. The user can click on this button to close the Web Assistant (both the *Carousel* and the *Help Stripe*). This is effectively the same as clicking on the **Help** button again, when the *Carousel* and/or *Help Stripe* is already displayed).

Specified as:

```
showCloseButton=[true|false]
```

showEnableNow

This parameter can be used to 'force' the display of the *Carousel*, even if SAP Enable Now has not been 'enabled' in the application (other parameters must still be specified).

Specified as:

```
showEnableNow=[true|false]
```

showMinimizeButton   *See page 199*

By default, the *Help Stripe* will include a **Hide** button at the bottom that can be used to hide the *Carousel* and leave only the *Help Stripe* displayed. (Clicking on the **Show** button [displayed when the *Carousel* is hidden] will re-display the *Carousel*.) If this parameter is set to **false** then the **Minimize** button is not shown.

Specified as:

```
showEnableNow=[true|false]
```

showShortDescription   *See page 197*

By default, Help Tiles will show the tile title, followed by up to four lines of short description. If this parameter is set to **false** then all tiles initially contain only the title, and the short description is only displayed when the user clicks on the tile (or the associated Hotspot).

Specified as:

```
showShortDescription=[true|false]
```

showWhatsNew   *See page 94*

When this parameter is set to **true**, the message `We have added some great new features. Click here to find out more.` is displayed at the top of the screen, as soon as the user accesses the application. (The message text is hard-coded and cannot be changed.)

Specified as:

```
showWhatsNew=[true|false]
```

themeBase

See page 183

Used to select the overall color scheme for the *Carousel* and *Help Stripe*. Almost all colors and accents can be overridden by specific individual parameters.

Specified as:

```
themeBase=[default|hcb|light|quartz|sfsf]
```

These values have the following effects:

Value	Effect
default	Dark gray tiles and white text, with green highlight/accents.
hcb	'High-contrast black': Black tiles and white text, with blue highlights/accents
hcw	'High-contrast white': White tiles and black text, with light blue highlights/ and orange accents.
light	Light gray tiles and black text, with green highlights/accents.
quartz	Dark blue tiles with white text, and light blue highlights/accents.
sfsf	Designed for SuccessFactors: Blue tiles and white text, with light blue highlights/accents

➕ **hcb** and **hcw** are not officially documented, but work, as of the time of writing. They may be announced for a future release.

tour

Deprecated. See **autoStartTour**.

trackingTokenWebAnalytics

Currently not supported. Presumably for future integration with SAP Web Analytics.

trackingUrlWebAnalytics

Currently not supported. Presumably for future integration with SAP Web Analytics.

trackingUrlWPB

See page 134

If Web Assistant content usage is to be recorded on the *Web Assistant Usage Report* then this parameter should specify the URL of the primary Workarea (usually the same Workarea as the one in which the learning content is located—not necessarily the one in which the help content is located).

Specified as:

```
trackingUrlWPB={URL of your Workarea}
```

uiBg

See page 190

Used to specify the color of the following elements:

- The background color of the *Carousel* (including the *Help Stripe*)
- The background color of Help Bubbles (including Guided Tours)
- The color of the *Carousel* scrollbar (derived from this color: the track is slightly lighter, and the control is slightly darker)

Specified as:

```
uiBg={R,G,B}
```

where {R,G,B} are the comma-separated decimal RGB values of the chosen color.

uiFg

See page 190

Used to specify the color of the following elements:

- Text and icons in tiles on the *Carousel* (unless hovered over—see **accentFg**).
- The border around the **Search** field
- The **Previous** and **Next** buttons in Guided Tours
- Guided Tour 'step type' texts (such as "Start Guided Tour")

Specified as:

```
uiFg={R,G,B}
```

where {R,G,B} are the comma-separated decimal RGB values of the chosen color.

✚ **updateInterval** was added in Version 2.4.10.

updateInterval

Used to specify the frequency with which the position of Hotspots on the application screen should be re-calculated: If the application screen can be rapidly scrolled, the Hotspots may briefly appear at the wrong position. Reducing the **updateInterval** can reduce this effect—but at the cost of increasing system load.

Specified as:

```
updateInterval=[{nn}|100]
```

where {nn} is the number of milliseconds between updates.

useGlobalHelp

This property is specific to support for SAPGui for HTML and WebDynpro apps running in the Fiori Launchpad. If no default Web Assistant content is available for these apps (as is usually the case) then setting this parameter to true will result in specific (pre-defined, built-in) help tiles being displayed that explain how to access help for the respective system.

If this parameter is set to **true** then the **noHelpMode** parameter should also be used, and set to carousel.

Specified as:

    useGlobalHelp=[true|**false**]

verticalW See page 197

Used to specify the width of the *Carousel* (excluding the *Help Stripe*, which is always 44 pixels wide), in pixels.

Specified as:

    useGlobalHelp=[{nn}|**280**]

where {nn} is the number of pixels.

whatsNewDirect See page 95

This parameter (when set to **true**) will cause the *Carousel* to be automatically opened and the *What's New* page displayed, as soon as the user accesses the application. If this parameter is specified then the **infoBarTimeoutWhatsNew** parameter is ignored (because the *What's New* page is already displayed). This parameter takes priority over the **showWhatsNew** parameter.

Specified as:

    whatsNewDirect=[true|**false**]

whatsNewExpiration See page 95

This parameter is used in conjunction with **whatsNewDirect**, and specifies the date after which the *What's New* page should not be automatically displayed when the user accesses the application.

Specified as:

    whatsNewExpiration={YYYY-MM-DD}

WNBg
See page 192

Used to specify the color of the following elements:

- Background color for hovered-over tiles on the *What's New* page of the *Carousel*
- The *What's New* page 'selector tab' in the *Help Stripe*.
- The border of Hotspots for 'What's New' help
- The title bar on Bubbles for 'What's new' help

(Effectively, this is the equivalent of **accentBg**, but for What's New.)

Specified as:

```
WNBg={R,G,B}
```

where {R,G,B} are the comma-separated decimal RGB values of the chosen color.

WNFg
See page 192

Used to specify the color of text and icons for hovered-over tiles on the *What's New* page of the *Carousel*, and the Title in What's New Bubbles. (Effectively, this is the equivalent of **accentFg**, but for What's New help content.)

Specified as:

```
uiFg={R,G,B}
```

where {R,G,B} are the comma-separated decimal RGB values of the chosen color.

Index

learningAppWorkspace parameter: 96, 205, 222
   Definition: 222
   Use: 44
Learning button: 163
Learning Center: 14, 130
   Button: 96
Learning Center button
   Description: 14
learningCenterUrl parameter: 96, 129, 137
   Definition: 222
   Use: 164
Learning Package
   Learning App Category: 161
Learning page
   Description: 13
Learning Tile
   Web Assistant: 95
Lightbox: 11, 78, 198
Lightbox Sizing: 79
Link
   Inserting into Bubble Text: 113
Link Tile
   Changing: 80
   Creating: 76
   Deleting: 81
   Description: 10
   Web Assistant: 76
Local Preview: 166
Local Trash: , 145
Logical Info Object property: 108

M

Macro Fallback Settings: 104
Macro Initialization: 104
mediaUrlUACP parameter
   Use: 44
Microsoft Azure: 34, 35, 223
Microsoft Excel: 137
Microsoft Word
   Translation File format: 177
Minimize button
   Showing or hiding: 199

N

NetWeaver: 36
newWindowSAML parameter
   Definition: 223

   Use: 36
noHelpMode parameter: 223, 229

O

Object Editor Pane: 144
Object Navigation Pane: 144
Offset
   For Bubble anchor point
      In Web Assistant: 86
Okta: 34, 35, 223
onHelpActive function: 206
onHelpAvailable function: 206, 223
onHelpBusy function: 206
onHelpCarousel function: 206
onHelpMinimized function: 206
onHelpMode function: 206
onHelpRequireIndent function: 199, 207
openImmediately parameter
   Definition: 224
Open in Lightbox: 79
Options button: 61
Orientation
   For Bubble
      In Web Assistant: 88
Other
   Learning App Category: 162

P

panelHeadlineFg parameter: 224
   Use: 192
PDF files: 153
PDF Files
   Link Tile: 78
Ping Federation: 34
Placeholder
   Inserting into Bubble Text: 115
Play Automatically
   Video: 121
Position property
   For Bubble
      In Web Assistant: 88
PowerPoint: 188
Processes
   Learning App Category: 162
Producer license: 18, 19
Product Name: 138, 159, 165
Product Name property: 156

Product property: 212
Product Version: 138, 159, 165
Product Version property: 156, 212
Project Explorer: 144
Published View: 166
Publish Help
   Web Assistant option: 98
Publish Tour
   Web Assistant option: 98

R

Rating: 140
readCatalogue parameter: 223
   Definition: 224
Recognition Information panel: 69, 210
Recognition Rule: 69, 208
Record Web Assistant Context: 153
Rectangle
   Hotspot Style: 72
Release Information: 64
Remove Help: 82
Remove Locally: 150
Remove Tour: 92
Remove Tour Extension: 92
Reports
   Exporting: 138, 139
   Generating: 134
   Subscribing: 140
Requested Language
   Help context: 176
Resources: 145
   Location of: 145
resourceUrl parameter
   Definition: 225
   Use: 36, 44
Revert all to Original: 82
Revert Object: 152
Role property: 162
Roles
   In Learning Center: 14
Root: 145

S

S/4HANA: 25, 29, 36, 37
   Standard Workarea: 31
SAML: 34, 218
saml2 parameter

Definition: 225
SAP Cloud Platform: 50
SAP Digital Manufacturing Cloud: 47
SAPGui: 229
SAP Integrated Business Planning: 47
SAP JAM: 15, 221
sap-language parameter: 173
SAP Marketing Cloud: 47
SAP S/4HANA Cloud: 47
SAPUI5: 43, 44
Scheduling
   Reports: 140
Screen
   Key property: 149
   Macro: 149
Select Macros By Type
   Function: 149
Send feedback to author button: 15
serviceLayerVersion parameter: 24, 128, 217, 218
   Definition: 225
   Use: 21, 44, 51
Settings macro: 101
SharePoint: 22
Show as Announcement: 80
Show Bubble Arrow property
   In Web Assistant: 88
showCloseButton parameter
   Definition: 225
   Use: 59, 199
showEnableNow parameter
   Definition: 226
Show in Manager Workspace button: 126
Show in Manager Workspace function: 129
showMinimizeButton parameter
   Definition: 226
   Use: 59, 199
showShortDescription parameter
   Definition: 226
   Use: 156, 198
Show Title Bar: 87, 88
Show Tree Operations: 161
showWhatsNew parameter: 229
   Definition: 226
   Use: 95
SID: 38
Simulation: 13
Simulation Project: 146
Skip Step on Missing UI Element: 89

W

X

Y

Z

www.ingramcontent.com/pod-product-compliance
Lightning Source LLC
Chambersburg PA
CBHW042320070326
40689CB00058B/4982